ENCYCLOPAEDIA OF EMINENT THINKERS

VOLUME-I: **MAHATMA GANDHI**

Encyclopaedia of Eminent Thinkers Series

Vol. I. The Political Thought of **Mahatma Gandhi**

Vol. II. The Political Thought of **Nehru**

Vol. III. The Political Thought of **Rabindra Nath Tagore**

Vol. IV. The Political Thought of **Radhakrishnan**

Vol. V. The Political Thought of **Vinoba**

Vol. VI. The Political Thought of **Aurobindo**

Vol. VII. The Political Thought of **Jayaprakash Narayan**

Vol. VIII. The Political Thought of **Vivekananda**

Vol. IX. The Political Thought of **Ambedkar**

Vol. X. The Political Thought of **M.N. Roy**

About the Author

K.S. Bharathi did his Master's Degree in Gandhian Thought, Peace-Science, Economics, and Political Science. He also did Postgraduate Diplomas in Politics, Public Administration, Population Dynamics, Gandhian Thought, Tourism, and Telgu. He has contributed some articles in learned journals. He is the author of : *Foundation of Gandhian Thought, Gandhi and Humanity, Socio-Religious Thoughts of Mahatma Gandhi, The Philosophy of Sarvodya, The Satyagraha of Mahatma Gandhi, Gandhi and Nehru, Foundations of Ambedkar Thought, The Social Philosophy of Mahatma Gandhi, Gandhian Approach to Rural Development, The Relevance of Gandhi, Gandhi and Vinoba, The Philosophical Foundations of Gandhian Thought, The Political Thought of Gandhi, The Economic Thought of Gandhi, The Social Thought of Gandhi,* and *The Quintessence and Chronology of Gandhi*. At present, he is the Head of the Postgraduate Department of Gandhian Thought of Nagpur University. He is the Chairman of the Board of Studies of Gandhian Thought, member of the Academic Council, member of the Faculty of Social Sciences, member of the Board of Examination, and member of the Doctoral Research Committee of Nagpur University.

Gandhian Studies and Peace Research Series – 11

ENCYCLOPAEDIA OF EMINENT THINKERS

VOLUME-ONE

THE POLITICAL THOUGHT OF MAHATMA GANDHI

K.S. BHARATHI
Head
P.G. Department of Gandhian Thought
Nagpur University, Nagpur

CONCEPT PUBLISHING COMPANY, NEW DELHI 110059

ISBN 81-7022-685-6 (Vol. 1)

ISBN 81-7022-684-8 (Series)

First Published 1998

Published and Printed by
Ashok Kumar Mittal
Concept Publishing Company
A/15-16, Commercial Block, Mohan Garden,
NEW DELHI-110059 (India)

Ph 5648039, 5649024
Fax 091-11-5648068

TO

PREETI

PREFACE

Gandhiji's political concepts possess a variety of meanings ranging from religious purity to political expediency, but he was neither a pure absolutist nor a mere opportunist in his interpretations of the terms he used. It would be a failure to grasp the man or his ethical preoccupations to explain away his concepts entirely in terms of political expediency. He certainly evolved his concepts and elaborated them in the context of practical problems that he faced as a politician and social worker.

Gandhiji's claim to be regarded as a political thinker lies in that he did give an account of the nature of political activity, presented a relationship between the activity and the moral nature of man, and gave a sketch of a set of criteria for the judgement of politics. But none of these attempts can be understood without descending into the depths of what Romain Rolland called the vast religious crypt below the edifice of his moral and political thought.

The life and works of Gandhi has been covered in the first chapter. Influences on Gandhi has been analysed in the second chapter. Leadership, Religion, and Stateless Society have been discussed in the next three chapters. *Satyagraha* in South Africa has been covered in the last chapter.

I would like to place on record my indebtedness to scholars and thinkers whose ideas enabled me to bring out this book. I gratefully acknowledge the scholars from whose works I have drawn citations viz. Dr. Gopinath Dhawan, Dr. Bimal Prasad, Dr. Bali, Dr. Saroj Malik, Dr. Raghavan Iyer, Dr. Datta, Dr. Lal Khanna and Dr. W.E. Milhmann. Besides I have made use of Gandhiji's own writings and related literature.

So far as the writing of this book is concerned whatever success I have achieved is due to the relentless efforts and encouragement of my friend, Dr. P.S.G. Kumar, Head, Department of Library and Information Science, Nagpur University. I express my sincere gratitude to him.

I express my sincere thanks to Shri P.N. Hardas and Shri S.T. Patale for their help and cooperation provided to me in the completion of this work.

I am indebted to Shri Ashok Mittal, M/s Concept Publishing Co. for publishing this book in such a short span of time. Finally I hold myself to blame for the errors and shortcomings if any. This work would not have been completed without the grace of Lord Venkateswara of Tirumala and Alamelu Thayar of Tiruchanur.

K.S. BHARATHI

CONTENTS

1

LIFE AND WORKS OF GANDHI

Gandhiji was a man of his time, a time which made him a historic personality. At a decisive phase in the development of his country he became the symbol, the concentrated expression of the longing of his people for freedom from oppression and exploitation, for national independence. And he showed the way. Against the imprint of the foreign colonial power, he recalled the Indian culture, tradition and religion and thereby developed the consciousness of national strength.He propagated the idea of national struggle, which helped, to a certain extent, to overcome the barriers of caste and language.

Gandhiji was a great man. By any reckoning, he is one of the few outstanding personalities of the world in this century. Between the middle of the nineteenth and that of the twentieth centuries the world has seen a galaxy of great men who influenced their age in different ways. But none of them made greater impact on the thinking and actions of men than Gandhiji. His ideas and deeds permeated the entire human community. He was essentially a man who would be counted in the ages to come with the Buddha and Christ. He was the greatest of the humanists that India presented to the world in modern times.

Gandhiji was not a philosopher in the academic sense of the term. His ideas cannot be classed with any of the well-known schools of Indian philosophy. He was a practical man. In advocating his philosophy of action, he always advised men to take into account the psychological fact of human nature. He had tremendous faith in the goodness of man.

Mohandas Karamchand Gandhi was born on 2 October, 1869, at Porbandar in a middle class family of 'Vaishya caste'. Porbandar, one of the Kathiawad districts, is a coastal city on the west of Gujarat. The Peninsula of Kathiawad, also known as Saurashtra, has been the home of a strong and sturdy people. They differ from the people of Gujarat, of which Kathiawad is a sub-province. The teachings of Buddha and Mahavira are much prevalent in this area. Uttamchand Gandhi, the grandfather of Mohandas, was in the beginning of his career an ordinary employee of the Rana of Porbander. He was a resolute, thoughtful and dutiful officer and by dint of merit rose to be Dewan. He was a self-respecting man, possessed remarkable organising ability and conducted state affairs with unstinted loyalty, absolute integrity and fearless independence.

Uttamchand Gandhi married twice. His first wife bore him four sons, and the second two, Karamchand alias Kaba and Tulsidas. Of these six sons, the fifth (Kaba Gandhi) succeeded at the age of twenty-five to the Dewanship of Porbandar on his father's retirement. Like his father, Kaba Gandhi was a resolute, loyal, impartial and absolutely incorruptible minister. He was truthful, brave and generous, but short-tempered. He did not like interference in his work and so he left the Dewanship of Porbandar. His brother Tulsidas succeeded him as Dewan of Porbandar. Kaba Gandhi lost three wives. He married for the fourth time when he was over forty. Two daughters survived the three wives. His fourth and last wife Putlibai bore him a daughter named Raliatbehn and three sons Laxmidas, Karsandas and the youngest, Mohandas.

Mohandas mother, Putlibai, stood for religious faith and devotion. She had strict attitudes to alcohol and tobacco. Daily prayers and precise fasts were her routine. She had deep faith in religion and never took her food without daily prayers. Mohandas inherited such qualities from her whose life was also founded on long struggles and experiments with truth. The impact of this remarkable lady (Putlibai) proved to be profound and ineffaceable on the character of Mohandas. He inherited his father's stubbornness, incorruptibleness and practical sense and mother's life of religion, devotion and ascetism. His life was influenced both by Jainism and Vaishnavism.

Mohandas had his primary and high school education at Rajkot. He was regular and punctual at his school. At the age of 12, he was shifted to the Alfred High School. He was a mediocre student, shy and slow to mix with others. Many years later, he recalled his past, saying 'my intellect must have been sluggish and my memory raw'. During his school days, be never told a lie to his teachers or others. He had a distaste for reading beyond his school books. He was greatly influenced by an ancient play 'Shravana Pitribhakti' portraying the boundless love of Shravana for his parents. Thereafter, obedience to parents became Mohandas motto. Further, a play about Harischandra influenced him to lead a truthful and sincere life. He resolved to follow truth and to go through all the ordeals Harischandra went through, although he did not believe that Harischandra was an historical character. Thus Shravana and Hariscandra became the loadstars of his character. From early boyhood, his young mind was experiencing a kind of spiritual bewilderment and groping which led him to try to read and understand *Manusmriti* which was amongst his father's collection.

Mohandas was married to Kasturiba at the age of thirteen. She was the daughter of Gokuldas Makanji, who was a close friend of Kaba Gandhi and was a merchant. As per the records, she was born in April 1869, being about six months older than Mohandas. Her mother's name was Vrajkuwar. Kasturibai was her third child. She was a lovely girl with black hair, fine nose, delicate lips, well-formed chin and dark large eyes. She wore bracelets, anklets, earrings, rings on her fingers and a nose-ring. By nature, she was quiet and self-possessed.

A Brahmin named Ladha Maharaj devotionally read the Tulsidas's *Ramayana* to Mohandas's father. Mohandas was profoundly influenced by it, and he regarded the *Ramayana* as the greatest book in all devotional literature. This did not mean that in boyhood he had any living faith in God. He was somewhat inclined towards atheism and agnosticism. But from the discourses his father had with the priests on other religions, he learnt to be tolerant to other religions, and from his mother he learnt to worship all gods.

Mohandas passed the Matriculation Examination in 1887 and joined the Samaldas College in Bhavnagar, where he found the studies difficult and the atmosphere uncongenial. Right from his childhood, he was religious and used to recite *Ramanama* to overcome fear. After his father's death, he was offered to take up his father's place in the State service,but he he wished that he would better become a Barrister. He was urged to study law in England. This was objected by his caste people. However, he pleaded for himself. His mother's objection to his going abroad was overcome by the son's solemn vow not to touch wine, women and meat. He was so determined on becoming a Barrister that even the formal excommunication from his caste would not deter him.

Mohandas sailed for London in 1888. His initial days in London was miserable and he took time to accustom himself to the new situation. Later on he remarked, 'I would continually think of my home and country. Everything was strange—the people, their ways and even their dwellings. I was a complete novice in the matter of English etiquette and continually had to be on my guard. There was the additional inconvenience of the vegetarian vow. Even the dishes that I would eat were tasteless insipid'. While in London he read a book on 'Plea for Vegetarianism' by Henry Stephen Salt. This made him a vegetarian not only by his vow taken before his mother but also by principle. From then, the spread of the message of vegetarianism became a mission for him. His involvement with the vegetarians made him more sociable and popular. He was introduced to one poet, Narayan Hemachandra. On his request, he began to teach English. He undertook the task of becoming an English gentleman, but maintained the disciplined life of a student.

Mohandas came across Theosophists who told him about *Bhagvad Gita*. Later in his life, *Gita* became a book of his daily reading. Once he said, 'when doubt hangs me, when disappointment stares me in the face and when I see not one ray of light on the horizon, I turn to the *Bhagvad Gita*, and find verse to comfort me, and I immediately begin to smile in the midst of overwhelming sorrow.' To him, the central theme of the *Gita* was that a balanced state of mind can be achieved by killing all passions and by renouncing desires, rather than objects. From this he deduced that the result of selfless detachment must be uttermost truth and non-violence. He believed that the *Gita* advocated the supremacy of moral power over physical force.

Mohandas started reading the *Bible* and took great interest in the *New Testament*, particularly the Sermon on the Mount. He was attracted by the teachings of Buddha through Edwin's Arnlod *The Light of Asia.* A friend recommended Carlyle's *Heroes and Hero Worship* which afforded him to know about Prophet Mohammed.

Gandhiji returned to India after the legal education in London. He decided to start his practice in Bombay, but could not make headway. Then he made efforts to establish himself as a lawyer in his native place, Rajkot. It was, at this juncture, that an offer came from Dadda Abdullah to proceed to South Africa on their behalf to instruct their counsel in a law suit. Thus, in April 1893, he sailed for South Africa without his family. He left for Pretoria.

Capital of Transvaal, where his presence was required in connection with the case. It was in South Africa that the shy, timid, inexperienced and unaided Mohandas came into clash with the forces that obliged him to tap his hidden moral resources and turn the misfortune into creative spiritual experiences. He came face to face with racial prejudices and other oppressive atmosphere. Indians were treated as slaves and servants.

On his way to Pretoria, from Durban, at Maritzberg railway station, Gandhiji was detrained from the first class compartment even though he was holding appropriate ticket. The train strode away and he was left alone on the platform. It was winter and severe cold. In that sleepless night, he determined to fight the indiscrimination and root out the social evils and suffer and amount of hardship. He decided to work for removing the racial discrimination and subordinated his legal practice to public work.

Regarding the legal issue for which he was summoned to South Africa, Gandhiji could successfully bring both the parties together for arbitration and he realised that the true function of a lawyer was to unite the parties driven apart. Bitter experiences of indignity and humiliation aroused the sense of social justice in him. He called for a meeting of Indian community in Pretoria and exhorted his countrymen to forget all distinctions of religion and caste and work for the welfare of the people. He also hinted to the miseries and problems caused by the discriminatory attitude of the English people and exhorted the need for ending such a treatment.

Gandhiji was about to sail back home when Natal Government proposed to introduce a Bill to defranchise Indians in South Africa. Heeding to the request of the Indians, he extended his stay in South Africa and enrolled himself as an advocate of the Supreme Court of Natal. During this time, he came under the influence of the book *Kingdom of God is Within You* by Tolstoy. Tolstoy pleaded for the refusal of military service and payment of taxes, rejected the concept of state and for the establishment of a non-violent society which is economically and politically decentralised. Though incidental, the reading of John Ruskin's *Unto this Last* in 1904 had tremendous influence in his life. The magic spell of this book made Gandhiji to put his theories into practice. He founded Phoenix settlement near Durban and Tolstoy farm. He translated Ruskin's and Plato, loved to quote Thoreau, admired Mazzini, read Edward Carpenter and in short, was familiar with the best intellectual knowledge of

Europe and America. He, who was 'Vaishnav' by birth, developed his gospel of *ahimsa* as the spirit of his religion. The influence of the *Upanishads* on him is also worthy of study. He read Max Muller's translation of the *Upanishads* for the first time in 1894 in South Africa.

The Boer war broke out in 1889. As a matter of duty and patriotism, Gandhiji advised the Indian community to support the British corps. In 1901, he attended the Calcutta session of the Indian National Congress and was satisfied over the resolution of South Africa. During the Zullu Rebellion in 1906, he stood loyal to British Empire and organised an Indian Ambulance Corps. He was happy that he and his men had to nurse the sick and dying Zulus whom the white doctors and nurses were unwilling to touch. During this period, he took the vow of *brahmacharya*, as he felt that true service to humanity could not be done honestly and sincerely unless one takes the life of *brahmacharya*.

Gandhiji introduced the non-violent but powerful revolutionary weapon called *Satyagraha* in response to the Black Act. The immigrants gave an ultimatum to General Smuts to repeal the Black Act before August 1908. In the absence of a positive response from General Smuts, certificates were burnt and Indians were now prepared to face imprisonment. All these events enabled the personality development of Gandhiji.

On return from duty in connection with the Zullu Rebellion, Gandhiji came to know the Draft Ordinance published in the Transvaal Government Gazette. This ordinance required all Indians to register with the authorities to surrender the old permits taking their finger and thumb impression. Every individual who failed to do so was to forfeit his right of residence in Transvaal. He formed a passive resistance association to oppose such a move.

Gokhale visited South Africa in 1911 and informed Gandhiji that the Union Government had promised to repeal the Black Act. Later, the Union Government went back on its promise which made the Indians more furious. Meanwhile, a judgement of Supreme Court ruled that only Christian marriages were legal in South Africa, thus turning at one stroke all Indian wedlocks as invalid. This issue prompted the women to come forward and join the struggle. The continuous struggle organised in the non-violent way bore its fruits when the issue was successfully settled.

Gandhiji finally returned to India in January 1915, not as a lawyer but as a well-experienced organiser in the cause of social justice and equality. The experiences of political struggle in South Africa widened his mental horizon and field of activity, promising India a ray of hope for the suppressed humanity. Between 1893 and 1914, he visited India occasionally and those visits helped to maintain the link with Indian leaders like Gokhale, Tilak, Ranade, etc.

Gandhiji was essentially a man of religion. He was not religious in the ordinary sense in which religion is understood in India. It was religion based on truth and love. That is why religion for him became the basis of all his activities, it became his philosophy of life, it functioned as a source of strength in him. He made it clear that religion in its real sense could become the basis of friendship among all mankind. He considered different religions as the different roads going towards the same destination. On the basis of his own experience and study of different religions he came to the conclusion that all religions were true and based on the same principles of truth and love. He emphasised repeatedly that religions were not separating men from one another but rather for binding them.

After returning from South Africa, Gandhiji spent the first year in India touring all over the country and studying it with 'his ears open but his mouth shut'. In 1917, the first *satyagraha* in India was launched at Champaran in Bihar state. The peasants were compelled by the landlords to cultivate indigo on 15 per cent of their lands and part with the whole crop for rent. He skilfully tackeld the problem in a non-violent way. The Government appointed a committee in which Gandhiji was also a member. On recommendations of the committee, a Bill was passed in favour of the tenant-farmers. Thus, the success of his first *satyagraha* was registered. This was followed by Ahmedabad Textile Mill workers strike on bonus issue. He advised the workers to go on strike and he also stipulated certain conditions. The strike went on for 21 days. During the strike, he initiated his maiden fast for three days and his intervention had the desired effects. The issue was soon settled amicably through arbitration.

Gandhiji's next *satyagraha* was in Kheda district of Gujarat. Due to the failure of crops, the farmers demanded certain tax concessions. Many leaders of national eminence participated in this *satyagraha* and finally the government suspended the revenue assessment for the poor farmers. This *satyagraha* paved the way to awaken the political conscience and made the government to realise the potentials of mass movement.

In 1919, the Rowlatt Act was enforced. This induced Gandhiji to involve himself actively. This Act was opposed by many leaders. They observed *hartal* on 6 April, 1919. The *hartal* was peaceful and successful. The ill-feelings of the people disappeared and the movement became more widely spread.

Gandhiji ardently worked for the Hindu-Muslim unity. He elucidated its value and importance through his various articles in *Young India.* He categorically remarked that only harmonious relationship between the various classes and caste could lead to the national integration, solidarity and prosperity. His eminence dominated the Indian political horizon from 1920 onwards. He gave a new thrust to Indian National Congress and made the politicians more active and positive revolutionaries. Gradually women also started participating in the national movement. He bridged the gulf between the intelligentsia and the masses and widened the concept of *Swaraj.* He became one with the nation and his life could be unmistakably identified with the Indian history.

Under Gandhiji's leadership, the Congress decided to boycott the election to be held in 1920. At the same time, Congress launched non-cooperation movement for securing *swaraj.* His exhortation had energised the people to be prepared for arrest, imprisonment or any other form of tortures for the cause of national freedom. However, the tempo of the movement was hampered in February 1922 due to the outbreak of violence in Chauri Chaura. Due to this incident, he suspended the civil disobedience movement. Taking advantage of the anti-climax, the British government arrested him. In September 1922, he decided to wear loin-cloth in order to identify himself with the millions of poor in India.

Gandhiji was sent to jail for six years in Yeravada. The news of his arrest and imprisonment magnified his image and reputation. He was released from the jail in February 1924 on medical ground. In 1925, he started writing *The Story of My Experiments with Truth* through *Young India.* The spell of eleven vows came from Yeravada jail. Since 1925, he continued to devote more attention to the Hindu-Muslim problem. Till 1928, he extensively toured and propagated the Constructive Programme. Under the leadership of Gandhiji, the Congress, in 1928, demanded *Poorna Swaraj.*

Till 1930, the manufacture of salt was a government monopoly. A 24-day march to the beach at Dandi was organised against the salt tax. On 6 April, 1930, Gandhiji picked up a lump of salt and broke the British law. He was arrested on 5 May, 1930, and Sarojini Naidu assumed the leadership. In 1931, he was released and an agreement known as Gandhi-Irwin Pact was reached.

The First Round Table Conference was held in 1931. Gandhiji placed the demands of the Congress. When the British government refused to accept the demands of the Congress, the civil disobedience movement was once again started. In 1932, the British government proposed to introduce, in the Constitution of India, a separate electorate not only for the Muslims but for the 'Untouchables' as well, thereby causing a permanent vivisection of the Hindu community. He decided to fast unto death. On reaching an agreement, replacing the separate electorate, he broke his fast. On 11 February, 1932, the first issue of *Harijan* was published. In September 1933, he visited Wardha. He tried to raise a fund for the Harijan. In May 1934, Congress was permitted by the Government to meet at Patna. He severed his official connection with the Congress and he wanted to devote his time to constructive work which was meant to achieve and maintain *Swaraj*.

By 1936, Gandhiji had almost settled in Sevagram. And therefore, Sevagram became the headquarters for his activity. In 1937, a National Conference on Education was held at Wardha which gave birth to 'Basic Education'. From 1937 onwards, the communal disharmony increased between Hindu and Muslim. Discontentment frequently discussed in all Congress sessions. He was deeply pained by the riots between these communities. He considered it as a threat against national integration and solidarity and therefore tried his best to bring communal harmony.

With the outbreak of Second World War, Gandhiji was dragged back into the political arena. In March 1939, he undertook a fast in protest against the breach of promise by Thakore Saheb of Rajkot to the Praja Parishad which had been carrying on the struggle for responsible government in the state. Within a few days of his fast, Thakore Saheb agreed to fulfil the promise. By 1940, an anti-war campaign was launched. Vinoba, who led that movement was imprisoned soon. Despite his arrest, the campaign gained momentum.

Gandhiji once again left the Working Committee as he wanted to pursue his strategy of non-violence for independence and development. He did not want India to become independent under the shadow of war while the extremist members of Congress were less considerate towards the non-violent means of achieving independence.

In 1942, the British Cabinet sent the Cripps Mission to India with the new constitutional proposal. Gandhiji adopted uncompromising attitude towards the proposals of the Cripps Mission because those proposals did not satisfy the demands of the Congress. Gradually national feeling aroused against British rule and got crystallised in their demand that 'Britain must abandon her hold on India'. The Quit India resolution was passed by AICC in August 1942. He addressed the Congress Committee in which he eloquently and emotionally propounded the slogan of 'Do or Die'. On 9 August, 1942, he was arrested and the Congress Committee was declared as unlawful organisation. His arrest led the mob burst into violence campaign and sabotage. He was more and more aggrieved and maintained that conquest policy should be unequivocally non-violent. Later, he resorted to 21 days fast.

In September 1945, Gandhiji went to Bombay with Pyarelal to meet Jinnah in order to find out a solution for united India. Jinnah was adamant for a separate nation for Muslim. Nehru's intervention in this regard was also without success. The Muslim League decided to celebrate 16 August, 1946 as 'Direct Action Day'. It witnessed a powerful outbreak of communal rioting. Gandhiji was deeply shocked. He felt his dream of *Swaraj* was dwindling. Yet he decided that all energies that he possessed should be thrown for the service of the people. He proceeded to Naokhali to hide himself in East Bengal until such time as the Hindus and Muslims learn to live together in peace and harmony. His ambition was to wipe out every tear from every eye.

Setting aside all other affairs, Gandhiji devoted himself whole-heartedly to his mission by holding prayer meetings, preachings to the people on fearlessnees and the need for truth and non-violence. By the second week of March 1947, he left Naokhali and reached Patna. In Bihar, he did the same as in Naokhali. By then, British government realised that there is no way out than giving freedom for India. It appointed a committee and proposed for an 'Interim Government' for India. On 22 March, 1947, Lord Mountbatten flew to India and immediately invited Gandhiji to come to Delhi.

Gandhiji desired an undivided free India, but due to the indomitable attitude adopted by the communal groups, partition became inevitable. On the day of Independence and partition, there were communal disturbances in some pockets of the country like Bengal, Bihar and Punjab. Though India became independent on 15 August, 1947, Gandhiji was not happy over the communal riots and tension mounting in various parts of the country. He spent the day on fasting and spinning. He could not rest even after attainment of freedom. He felt that his words had ceased to be cared. He observed that the Congress was being corrupted by power. As such he wanted its dissolution and convert it as 'Lok Sevak Sangh'.

Though Gandhiji ardently worked for the Hindu-Muslim unity, his effort was misunderstood. The Hindu extremists were not ready to appreciate the success of his fast and they felt that Gandhiji had pledged the Hindu conscience to appease the Pakistanis. On the second day of the fast, an attempt was made on his life by throwing bomb. Though he escaped, he was not moved, but continued his discourse.

On 30th January, 1948, at one prayer meeting, Gandhiji was assassinated by a Hindu, Nathuram Vinayak Godse. He fell down on the ground uttering the words 'Heh Ram'. Thus, the apostle of non-violence had fallen a victim to violence. On the evening of 31th January, 1948, his body was reduced to ashes on the banks of Jamuna. The sad news of his assassination was conveyed to the country by Jawaharlal Nehru over the All-India Radio. He said, 'The light has gone out of our lives and there is darkness everywhere'. Our beloved leader, Bapu as we call him, the father of our nation, is no more. The light has gone out, I said, and yet I was wrong. The light that shown in this country was no ordinary light. The light that has illuminated this country for these many years and a thousand years later that light will still be seen in this country and the world will see it and it will give solace to innumerable hearts'.

The Danish Premier, M. Hans Bedtoft, said that Mahatma Gandhi represented to Danes the 'real idealist'. Prime Minister of Pakistan, Liaquat Ali Khan, sent Nehru their deepest sympathy over the tragic death of Gandhi. His dastardly assassination, he added, must be condemned unreservedly by everybody. President Truman of the U.S.A. said: 'As a teacher and leader, his influence made itself felt not only in India but everywhere in the world, and his death brings great sorrow to all peace-loving people'. George Marshall, U.S. Secretary of State, described Gandhi as a spokesman for the conscience of all mankind.

Gandhi as a Political Philosopher

Gandhiji was the greatest Indian since Buddha. He realised a task which was considered almost impossible of fulfilment. Through the use of the techniques of creative love and moral resistance and the mobilisation of mass resources through the application of the Constructive Programme he led four hundred millions to the path of glorious independence. He, thus created one of the greatest convulsions in history and became an acknowledged architect of political freedom.

History is a witness to many distinguished philosophers, scientists, poets, statesmen, saints and political leaders in the world who have made significant contributions in their respective fields. Gandhiji was one among them. He was a great statesman and a rare man with rare qualities. During the last few decades there have been enormous developments in science and technology which have practically changed the face of the earth. But in spite of the great achievements in science and technology, we find that there prevails a certain chaos and confusion at all levels.

We see people going from bad to worse every day. There is confusion and anarchy at all levels of human existence. Hypocrisy dominates the present day world. Every great leader of the world talks of peace but behind this talk, there is preparation for war. Under such circumstances, it seems to us that we have to fall back upon the Gandhian philosophy. We are, therefore, firmly of the opinion that there is no other way but to accept and adopt the principle of Gandhian thought. This could be possible only if Gandhian principles of life are strictly adhered to. Those who subscribe to Gandhian ideals hold that, under the present circumstances, the Gandhian principles of life are the only remedy for all evils. It is only through the cultivation of those principles that the salvation of mankind is possible.

Political thinkers are properly studied without undue reference to their personalities. When we turn to Gandhi's political concepts, we find it difficult to ignore his personality and his activities. More books and essays have already been written about Gandhi than about any other figure in world history except the founders of the great religions. No one else has ever been compared to such a wide range of historical personages. Gandhiji has been vividly portrayed as a saint by Romain Rolland, Carl Heath and Stanley Janes, a portrait confirmed by those who were closest to him. Gandhiji himself disclaimed the appellations of saint, ascetic, *sannyasi* and *Mahatma*, and described himself simply as one who claims only to be a humble searcher after truth.

Gandhiji stressed that he was an ordinary man who evolved by setting himself seemingly impossible standards. He identified himself completely with the poor and the weak, with *Daridra-narayan*. The image of Gandhiji as a politician is even more puzzling than the image of him as a saint. He has been aptly described as a hyphen connecting the middle classes and the people which transferred energy from each to the other. He himself claimed that the politician in him had never dominated a single decision of his that he had sacrificed no principle to gain a political advantage, that he was used to misrepresentation all his life, that there was a consistency running through his seeming inconsistencies, that his leadership was not of his seeking but a fruit of faithful service, that he was a practical dreamer but not a visionary.

Gandhiji was not a politician in the sense that he might well have failed in the practical business of government and that he never sought or held any political office—not even the official leadership of any party. Politics was to him not a profession but a vocation, and he was a politician only in the sense that he was conscious of a mission to serve the masses in the political sphere and to inspire them with a love of the common ideal. To grasp his political thought, it is not necessary to come to a firm view about Gandhiji's personality, as a saint or a politician, a saintly politician or a political saint.

There are several reasons why Gandhiji has not been regarded as a political thinker by many who have written about him. The personality of the man has attracted so much attention that his voluminous writings have been neglected. There has been a natural but undue concentration upon the image of the politician and reformer formed during his active phase of over thirty years in India, from 1914 to 1948. He was not an intellectual in the conventional sense. His political thought is so closely bound up with religious and ethical beliefs that several writers have concentrated upon the latter to the exclusion of the former.

Gandhiji, like the religious prophets but unlike most political thinkers, was concerned that after his death some would ascribe a literalness and finality to his entire body of statements that he never intended. He once told the Gandhi Seva Sangh, 'Let Gandhism be destroyed if it stands for error. Truth and *ahimsa* will never be destroyed, but if Gandhism is another name for sectarianism, it deserves to be destroyed. If I were to know, after my death, that what I stood for had degenerated into sectarianism, I should be deeply pained. . . . Let no one say that he is a follower of Gandhi. It is enough that I should be my own follower.... You are no followers but fellow students, fellow pilgrims, fellow seekers, fellow workers'.

It is apt to concentrate upon Gandhiji's concepts of conscience and heroism, tolerance and civility, *satya* and *asatya*, *ahimsa* and *himsa*, *moksha* and *tapas*, *satyagraha*, *swaraj* and *swadeshi*. All these concepts are based upon metaphysical presuppositions, but they have important ethical and political implications. He never claimed to be, and certainly cannot be regarded as, a well-trained intellectual, but this does not mean that he was not an original thinker. His reading, especially on morals and politics, was greater and wider than is usually realised, though less systematic than that of the other leading Indian intellectuals of his generations. It is hardly surprising that no other Indian politician or religious man became as original in his thinking as Gandhiji. The enormous importance of his metaphysical presuppositions to a grasp of his moral and political ideas imparts a classical flavour to his thought.

All sorts of political labels have been applied to Gandhiji—individualist, anarchist, socialist, communist, liberal, reactionary, revolutionary, nationalist, cosmopolitan and so on. His political concepts possess a variety of meanings ranging from religious purity to political expediency, but he was neither a pure absolutist nor a mere opportunist in his interpretations of the terms he used.

It is important to see that Gandhiji was merely a political moralist who wrote from the standpoint of the rebel, who did not concern himself with the ethical and practical problems facing men in authority. He was a man of action rather than an abstract theorist. He tried to apply his baisc concepts of *satya* and *ahimsa* to a variety of practical matters—the relation between capital and labour, the decentralisation of economic and political power, social inequalities and different types of exploitation, the connection between individual liberty and national independence, the promotion of collective welfare and village self-government, attitudes toward work and the problem of full employment, the alienation of the intelligentsia and the universal obligation of manual labour, the problems of educational and social reconstruction. His ideas have considerable relevance to the societies of the future. His political vision was ultimately based upon the classical Indian myth of *Ram Rajya*.

Gandhiji was deeply concerned to transcend the limitations of time and space and to view political society subspecie aeternitatis in the classical tradition of political thought. To quote Raghavan Iyer—

> "Early in life, Gandhi reacted strongly against modern civilisation and saw a contradiction between our deepest moral values as individuals and the materialistic criteria by which we tend to judge our institutions and our collective progress. He thought that the sickness of modern civilisation is reflected in our soulless politics, owing to a segregation between religion and politics and the prevalent doctrine of double standards. He redefined both religion and politics so as to emphasise the distinction between sectarian beliefs and religious commitment, between power politics and pure politics. Politics is corrupted by power-seeking and it could be purified by introducing the monastic ideal into the sphere of political activity and social service. All men must come to accept certain moral values as absolute, especially truth and non-violence. At least, some men must pledge themselves by vows to upholding these absolute values in public life. The reason for such drastic remedies is that human nature is so constituted that it must either soar or sink, and it will increasingly connive at untruth and violence if the quest for self-perfection is abandoned. Individuals should not abdicate from social responsibilities in their quest for personal salvation. It is possible to combine an appeal to conscience with heroic action in the midst of society, to yoke freedom with commitment."

Gandhiji did not produce a treatise embodying his considered political thought, but one can gather it from his prolific writings and recorded speeches. What he wrote and spoke, founded on his experiments with truth and non-violence, constitute his earnest plea to humanity to tread firmly the path of love. While the Gandhian movement in India aimed at political freedom of the country, it remained intensely spiritual. Its ultimate aim was to secure the absolute freedom for the individual. While Gandhiji was outwardly a politician par excellence, he was inwardly completely spiritual.

Gandhiji stood for the welfare of all. The concept of Sarvodaya, which he propounded, is superior to the Benthamite doctrine of 'the greatest good of the greatest number'; he wanted the greatest good of all. It is possible only if man gives up exploitation of man. Enjoining the people to build a non-exploitative society, he stressed that it should be free from these seven ills: politics without conscience, knowledge without character, commerce without morals, science without humanity, and worship without sacrifice. The ideal, as Gandhiji himself conceded, is not realisable; he thought it was like Euclid's point. Though utopian, it shows the way. Progressive practice of love takes the people nearer to peace.

Gandhiji did not consider political philosophy as a distinct, autonomous intellectual system separated from ethics, economics, sociology, etc. He viewed life in its totality. He looked at life on face, not in profile. For Gandhiji, therefore, there was no line of demarcation between economics and ethics, ethics and politics, politics and economics, etc. This might have been due to the influence of the Indian philosopher tradition. Every problem is discussed by the Indian philosopher from all possible approaches—metaphysical, ethical, logical, etc.

Regarding the elements in political philosophy, Prof. C. Wright Mills observed:

> "A political philosophy is itself a social reality; it is an ideology in terms of which certain institutions and practices are justified and others attacked; it provides the phrases in which demands are raised, criticisms made, exhortations delivered, proclamations formulated, and at times, policies determined. Secondly, it is an ethic, an articulation of ideals which on various levels of generality and sophistication is used in judging men, events, and movements, and as goals and guidelines for aspirations and policies. Thirdly, it designates agencies of action, of the means of reform, revolution or conservation. It contains strategies and programmes that embody both ends and means. It designates, in short, the historical lovers by which ideals are to be won or maintained after they have been won. Lastly, it contains theories of man, society and history, or atleast assumptions about how society is made up and how it works; about what are held to be its most important elements and how these elements are typically related; its major points of conflict and how these conflicts are resolved. It suggests the methods of study appropriate to its theories. From these theories and with those methods, expectations are derived."

As a practical man, Gandhiji was concerned with taking care of the present. One step was enough for him. He said, 'I know only the moment's duty'. This pragmatic approach characterises his political philosophy. His political philosophy, like any other political philosophy, at, once provides specific answers for specific situations and contains general principles of an enduring nature. One must try to be careful enough to distinguish between these elements so that there be no distortion in a balanced evaluation of their relative importance.

Gandhiji stressed some fundamental ideas for the regeneration of man and the reconstruction of society and politics, and in this sense he can be regarded as a moral, social and political thinker. He only stressed certain basic values and did not systematically elaborate the underlying philosophical assumptions and the sociological, political and economic implications of his theories. He was a genius not of the intellect but of the spirit. Gandhism only signifies the reaffirmation of the old spiritual truths substantiated by the concrete social-political experiments and the intense subjective *sadhana* of Gandhiji himself. It is not a systematic well-worked out political philosophy with explicity and rationally clarified theoretical assumptions and clearly drawn out social and political propositions therefrom.

Gandhiji was a man of action and a leader who wielded considerable influence over men. He cannot be considered a systematic social and political philosopher of the type of Plato and Hegel. He was modest enough not to claim to have originated any new system of philosophy or political thought. He has expressed many ideas which are highly useful and relevant to the modern age. He practised the principles but put forward by him and, hence, there is power of profound appeal in his writings. He is intensely self-conscious and always in his books and articles there is repeated reference to his personal experiences.

Gandhiji combined both moral idealism and political success. He was not only a great figure in world history but also an angelic prophet. He was the combination of a God-seeking mystic and a moral dictator wielding political power by love. He is an example of the combination of goodness and greatness. He was a great nationalist leader, but political opportunism and personal self-seeking had no place in his life. The resort to lies, intrigues and conspiracies was not inserted in his political dictionary. He appeared as a political captain for the cause of distressed and embarrassed Indians, in South Africa, and on a far grater scale, in India. He was not merely a politician or a statesman, but a prophet and a seer of humanity.

The uniqueness of Gandhiji's leadership lay in his successful application of the techniques of non-violent *Satyagraha* to the political and social spheres. The South African *Satyagraha* was the first example of the political application of non-violence on a great scale. He triumphed as the political leader of the semi-starved people of India, and as the concrete embodiment of the aspirations of the mute millions. He will go down in history as the chief architect and builder of Indian independence. He claimed to be the leader not merely of the feudal aristocrats or the middle-class intellectuals and the bourgeoisie, but of the entire Indian population. His heart always had the interests of the 'dumb millions' as the prime consideration, and the village was always the centre of his attention.

Gandhiji did not claim any deep and profound learning in the ancient Sanskrit texts which was the great asset of Dayananda and Tilak. His powers as an orator were also considerably limited. His speeches were severely simple, direct and pointed. He was able, nevertheless, to acquire an amazing hold over Indian public opinion. The pettiest details about his life, movements and actions were flashed in the press. A vast section of the Indian people idolized him. His leadership was the consequence of his prolonged dedication to the cause of the people. His leadership was unique because to his political eminence he added the profundity of a saint and his message to the Indian people became so appealing because he simultaneously utilised the techniques of political and prophetic leaders. He always remained the simple, lovable, reasonable and sympathetic soul. The great secret of his influence was that he appeared to the Indian masses as a political leader giving hints of spiritual power. He was a saint who wanted to atone for his own sins and faults. His power was not due to his being a representative of the ecclesiastical and traditional forces of Hindu society. He built the foundations of his leadership through great suffering. His power and authority were really 'charismatic' because they were based upon his own moral and spiritual discipline. He rose to eminence by dint of tenacious loyalty to spiritual principles and self-confidence and his leadership was attained through heroic sufferings in the path of what he regarded as the divine way.

Gandhiji was one of the greatest embodiments of the old Indian values of spirituality, morality, austerity and devout saintliness. His leadership was reinforced by his spiritual personality. He pleaded for the incorporation of moral and spiritual values in politics. He rose to success by adopting the vows of voluntary poverty and austerity. His leadership was based on self-abnegation. He was neither a visionary, nor a utopian philosopher, nor a theoretical conceptualist. He was a *Karmayogi.*

Gandhiji had the noble attributes of a teacher and prophet of mankind and hence Romain Rolland regarded him as the Saint Paul of our times. He heralded a moral dispensation for a tormented humanity and hence he was much more than the liberator of a country. By his insistence on the negation of politics of power and the application of purity to politics, Gandhiji has restressed the aspiration of the noble humanity of all ages. He stood for realisation of the values of uprightness, candour and purity even in political conduct. He showed an unwavering resolve to apply only methods of civility and gentleness against his most ruthless political antagonists. He had the spiritual vision of the unity of all mankind and also believed in the ideal of world federation. He has taught the ideal of perfection of character.

As a political philosopher, Gandhiji emphasised the idealistic approach to politics. He fought for the rights and the dignity of the individual and eloquently championed the concept of resistance to unjustified authority. To him, the human soul is never to compromise with evil or injustice or with any concentration of irresponsible power. His advocacy of *Satyagraha* against the monopolization of coercion and constraint by the state and other engines of repression is a great and noble antidote to all those political philosophies which stand for militant political realism and sponsor the power of the 'Prince' or the leviathan or the determinate human superior or the totalitarian structure with the absolute command over political and economic resources.

To quote Romain Rolland, "For if there is such a thing as genius, great by its own strength whether or not it corresponds to the ideals of its surroundings, there can be no genius of action, no leader, who does not incarnate the instincts of his race, satisfy the need of the hour, and requiet the yearning of the world. Mahatma Gandhi does all this". It was because Gandhi could realise the historical necessity and evolve a technique which could rouse the masses into action that he earned the supreme leadership of the nation.

Gandhiji emphasised that moral regeneration was essential even for political and social betterment. The Gandhian political philosophy represents a synthesis of the spiritual and the mundane. If on one side it has its eyes fixed upon the eschatological conception of the salvation of the human soul, it is, on the other side, no less emphatic in its urgent appeal for bettering the economic and social conditions of the Indian villages by stressing the use of *Khadi* and the practice of the rules of hygiene and cleanliness. He represents a reaction against civilisation, its sophistries and its ostentations, and its maximisation of luxuries and pleasure. He is a champion of nationalism. He upholds the cause of moral authority in politics. He has a distrust of the action of the government. He is opposed to social and economic exploitation. He preaches the orientation of individual claims and rights to the realisation of the notion of the common rational good of all men. He vindicates the right of resistance against unjustified authority.

The political philosophy of Gandhiji has its basic roots in his studies of the *Bible* and the *Gita* and his own institutions and spiritual perceptions. He did not cast his views in clear-cut, rigid, logical categories but made suggestions to solve immediate problems. Gandhism in not a finished and closed system of thought. It can adjust itself to the demands of the times. The great merit of Gandhism is that being a synthetic and comprehensive system of social and political philosophy it can incorporate newer elements from other kindred systems of thought. It is not a system of dogmatic, closed, scholastic political thought. It reinforces the valuational and taleological approach to politics. Gandhiji's political philosophy makes an appeal to the values of the human personality in an age when the dignity, worth and sacrosanct character of man has been and might again be rudely and savagely attacked by the extraneous might of the weapons of mass destruction.

Gandhism wants to bring about a moral transformation in human society. It aims to substitute coercion as the dominant technique of political action by the supremacy of self-suffering love. It stresses the replacement of conflict, discord, barbarity and pugnacity by freedom, will and right. It upholds the replacement of the vulgarity of force by the authentic power of the changed human heart. Gandhiji is pessimistic of mere institutional changes and so, he places great emphasis on moral education, inner purification through the practice of the moral vows and the transfiguration of the soul. He is a prophet of the inner conscience and the internal light and the superiority of the moral quest.

2

ON INFLUENCES

Gandhiji was very much influenced by John Ruskin's *Un To This Last* book. He determined to change his life style according to the ideals of this book. He read the book in a journey from Johannesburg to Durban and he could not get sleep that night. He translated it later into Gujarati, entitling it, *Sarvodaya*. He said, "The book was impossible to lay aside once I had begun it. It gripped me. I could not get sleep that night. I determined to change my life in accordance with the ideals of the book".

John Ruskin, upholding the dignity of man, stressed that whatever hurts it must be relentlessly rejected. He thought that political economy took no account of the spirit of man and it concentrated on the material aspect of human welfare. He, therefore, attacked the mammon worship in society. He thought that riches were a power like that of electricity, acting through inequalities or negations of itself. That country, he emphasised, was the richest which nourished the great number of noble and happy human beings; that man was the richest, who, having perfected the functions of his own life to the utmost, had also the widest helpful influence, both personal and by means of his possessions, over the lives of the others; there was no wealth but life. He had no hesitation in coming to the irrefutable conclusion that true economics was the economics of justice. He believed in the eternal superiority of some men to others, sometimes even of one man to all others and approved the advisability of appointing such person or persons to guide, to lead, or on occasions even to compel and subdue their inferiors according to their own letter, knowledge and wiser will. He did not accept Ruskin's advocacy of the rule of the wisest.

Gandhiji reduced the teachings of *Un To This Last* into three principles:

1. That the good of the individual is contained in the good of all.
2. That a lawyer's work has the same value as the barber's inasmuch as all have same right of earning their livelihood from their work.
3. That a life of labour, i.e. the life of the tiller of the soil and the handicraftsman is the life worth living.

Gandhiji resembles Ruskin in several respects. Both preach the supremacy of the spirit and trust in the nobleness of human nature; to both character is more important than intelligence; both seek to moralise politics and economics; both emphasise the priority of social regeneration to mere political freedom; both greatly distrust machinery and plead that if employed at all, it should be so used as to free and not enslave men; both insist that the capitalist should adopt a wise paternal attitude in relation to his employees.

However, there are significant points of difference, and even contrast between both. Unlike Gandhiji, Ruskin did not believe in non-violence, democracy and equality. Gandhiji differed from Ruskin in his distrust of the people and in his belief in the rule of the wisest. Both disagreed in their views regarding the nature and functions of the State.

Gandhiji has drawn inspiration on education from Ruskin. For, both of them attach primary importance to education in their constructive programmes. According to them, education is the discipline of the inherent instinct of man. Both took into consideration the child's essential nature and emphasised that education must begin with the child. Both of them laid much stress on home. Ruskin regarded individual taste, national character and all those things which arose from national character as reflections of home life. Gandhiji also stressed the home education. Both attached equal importance to the education of boys as well as of girls. Both were of the opinion that spirit was higher than matter, both of them tried to spiritualise the political, economic and social spheres of human life.

The writings of Ruskin made Gandhiji to realise the dignity of labour and the ideal that action for the good of all is the most virtuous principle. Ruskin's *Un to This Last* left such and abiding impact on Gandhiji's life and thought that he started experimenting the philosophy contained therein, in his own life, renounced property and privileges, established socialist colonies thereafter, thought in terms of *Sarvodaya* and gave to the translation of the book, the title of *Sarvodaya*. Under the impact of Ruskin's book, Gandhiji equally believed that differential wage should not be paid for intellectual work in preference to manual work since intellectual labour should not be treated as superior to manual labour.

Gandhiji was influenced by the ideas and activities of Henri David Thoreau, the well known American Anarchist who refused to pay taxes as a protest against slavery in America. Thoreau's plea for the supremacy of conscience under all circumstances appealed to Gandhiji so much that he admitted that his technique of passive resistance found scientific confirmation in the former's essay on 'Civil Disobedience'. The core of Thoreau's politics was his belief in a natural or higher law. He rejected the idea that the highest responsibility of the individual must be to the State. He refused to recognise a government, which failed to establish justice in the land.

The anarchist view of Gandhiji was fully supported by Thoreau's declaration that 'that government is best which governs the least'. Gandhiji believed that a free and enlightened State could be established on this planet if its inhabitants could be truthful and non-violent in thought, word and deed.

Thoreau was the first to use the term, 'Civil Disobedience' in one of his speeches in 1849. Gandhiji, however, did not derive his idea from the writings of Thoreau. He wrote, 'The statement that I had derived my idea of Civil Disobedience from the writings of Thoreau is wrong. The resistance to authority in South Africa was well advanced before I got the essay of Thoreau on Civil Disobedience. I began the use of his phrase to explain our struggle to the English readers. But, I found that even Civil Disobedience failed to convey the full meaning of the struggle. I, therefore, adopted the phrase of 'Civil Disobedience'. Thoreau believed in man's natural impulses to goodness, argued for the supremacy under all conditions of conscience and held up the ideal of a future society without any government".

Thoreau's primary contribution to the realm of thought is his plea for defiance of a state based on injustice. A champion of the dignity of man and liberty of the individual, he would sweep aside, the obstacles, preventing fulfilment of their personality. He advocated a just, social and political order devoid of exploitation in form of slavery. He viewed that the poverty of the poor was the direct consequence of the luxury of the rich. He said, "Perhaps it will be found that just in proportion as some have been placed in outward circumstances above the savage, others have been degraded below him. The luxury of one class is counter-balanced by the indigence of another. On the one side is the palace on the other are the alms house and 'Silent Poor'. The myriads who built the pyramids to be the tombs of the Pharaohs were fed on garlic, and it may be were not decently buried. The mason who finishes the cornice of the palace returns at night perchance to a hut not so good as a wingman. It is a mistake to suppose that in a country where the usual evidence of civilisation exist, the condition of the very large body of the inhabitants may not be as degraded as that of savages".

Thoreau's message is contained in his saying 'if thy hand has plenty, be liberal as the date-tree; but if it affords nothing to give away, be an *azad* or freeman like the Cyprus'. He advocated service to fellow beings which may lead to renunciation. He was convinced that every one should earn his bread by his own labour. His very thesis that one can produce his own food for the year only by working for six weeks is a hint that earning one's bread by physical labour is a philosophy that covers even intellectual.

Tolstoy lifted Christianity from the traditional ruts and gave it a spiritual meaning. Gandhiji said, "It was forty years back when I was passing through a severe crisis of skepticism and doubt that I came across 'The Kingdom of God is within You', and was deeply impressed by it. I was at that time a believer in non-violence. Its reading cured me of my skepticism and made me a first believer in *Ahimsa*. What has appealed to me in Tolstoy's life is that he practised what he preached and reckoned to cost too great in his pursuit of truth". Again, "He was the greatest apostle of non-violence that the present age has written and spoken on non-violence so fully or so insistently and with such penetrations and insight as he. I would even go further and say that his remarkable development of this doctrine puts to shame the present day narrow and lop-sided interpretation put upon it by the votaries of *Ahimsa* in this land of ours".

The book *The Kingdom of God is Within You* captivated Gandhiji very much. Tolstoy appreciated the non-violent struggle led by Gandhiji. Gandhiji accepts the influence of Tolstoy. He said,

"I made too an intensive study of Tolstoy's books, *The Gospel In Brief*, *What To Do*? and such other books made a deep impression on me. I began to realise more and more the infinite possibilities of universal love". He not only conquered with the belief of Tolstoy that "The Kingdom of God is Within You", but realised it in his life by strenuous endeavour. His successful striving after truth was an eloquent demonstration of the Tolstoyan declaration that "The Kingdom of God can only be reached by effort and only those who make such effort reach it".

Gandhiji agreed with Tolstoy's reminder to the mass of humanity, in the language of Christ, that "We are all sons of one father, no matter where we live or what language we speak; we are all brothers and are subject only to the law of love, which the common father has implanted in our hearts". Tolstoy pointed to the division of men into castes: one labouring, oppressed, needy and suffering; the other idle oppressing and living in luxury and pleasure. Gandhiji upheld the Tolstoyan dictum that an ideal state would be an ordered anarchy, in which everyone would rule himself in such a manner that he would never be a hindrance to his neighbours.

Love is the basis of Tolstoy's principles of non-resistance and non-cooperation. He asserts, in his 'Three Parables', that 'Evil must not be driven out within evil, that all resistance by violence merely increases the evil'. Tolstoy's philosophy of Christian anarchism repudiates the authority of the state and private property, for they are based on physical balance. His philosophy is the application of the teaching of the *Sermon on the Mount*. To Tolstoy, the *Sermon on the Mount* which contains the essence of Christianity, teaches us to live in peace with all men, to harbour anger towards none, and to love all men alike without distinction of nationality.

Gandhiji's conception of non-violence is slightly different from that of Tolstoy. To Tolstoy, non-violence means avoidance of the force in all its forms and in all circumstances. But for Gandhiji in certain circumstances, even killing may be called *ahimsa*, as life involves some amount of violence. He follows the *Gita's* ideal of action and resists evils with the detachment of spirit. Gandhiji excels Tolstoy in working out the non-violent technique and in devising ways to remove social evils.

Tolstoy was the great apostle of *ahimsa*. His penetration into the efficacy of this weapon was deep. None in the West has so fully read and understood about *ahimsa* as Tolstoy. J.J. Doke is of the opinion that the miscellaneous writings of Tolstoy especially on ethical, religious and allied problems were traced out, read and digested by Gandhiji. He calls him a disciple of Tolstoy. Gandhiji wrote his first letter to Tolstoy in October, 1909. In his letter he described the passive resistance which was going on in Transvaal for three years. Tolstoy replied to this letter of Gandhiji, addressing Transvaal Satyagrahis as 'dear brothers and co-workers'. In 1910, Gandhiji laid the foundation of Tolstoy farm which was to become a laboratory for experiments on the philosophy and teachings of passive resistance.

Tolstoy condemns the State and its machinery, law courts, police and military, private property and capitalism, even the schools, as all these offend against the law of love. He is opposed to the use of force, payment of taxes, and compulsory military service. He lays great stress on the moral regeneration of the individual.

Tolstoy and Gandhiji are seekers of truth. Both denounce modern civilisation based on force and exploitation. Both oppose the violent methods of fighting evil. Both lay stress on the reform of the individual, his inner self-perfection for social regeneration. Both concern with the purity of means. Both advocate an ascetic morality and preach extreme simplicity of life, bread-labour and virtual celibacy as being essential for the moral growth of the individual.

There are some facts which differentiate Gandhiji from Tolstoy. Gandhiji is more practical than Tolstoy. He used to make compromises on matters relating to principles. Gandhiji's idea of non-violence is slightly different from that of Tolstoy. Gandhiji defined *Ahimsa* in the sense of avoidance of injury to any creature out of anger, Tolstoy took *Ahimsa* in the sense of avoidance of force in all forms. As life involves violence, Tolstoy turns away from it; Gandhiji, on the other hand, followed the *Gita* ideal of action which preaches action without attachment. Gandhiji did not accept Tolstoy so far as the question of reincarnation is concerned. Gandhiji wrote to Tolstoy, "Reincarnation or transmigration is a cherished belief with millions in India, indeed, in China also. With many, one might almost say, it is a matter of experience, no longer a matter of academic acceptance. It explains reasonably the many mysteries of life". Gandhiji did not find anything new in Tolstoy. Therefore, he said, "There is no doubt that there is nothing new in what Tolstoy preaches. But his presentation of the old truth is refreshingly forceful. His logic is unassailable. And, above all, he endeavours to practise what he preaches. He preaches to convince. He is sincere and earnest. He commands attention".

Tolstoy had renounced the happy and go-lucky life addicted to luxury, lived the life of a poor peasant, swept and cleaned his own room, his clothes and shoes, worked with peasants in his own estate Yasnaya Polyanna, ploughed and furrowed the land, worked for peasant families who were running short of labour, and sometimes performed all the farm operations for a poor widow, who could hardly afford to engage hired labourers. This life of renunciation and dedication to the service of the poor and the oppressed had such a great appeal for Gandhiji that he refashioned his life accordingly. He renounced his property and embraced voluntary poverty, clothed himself like a poor peasant, made ample use of his limbs to earn his bread and travelled in third class railway compartments after he opted for a life of renunciation. To quote Pyarelal, "It was not Tolstoy's writings alone, but the example of his life, his passion for truth and ceaseless striving after perfection that enthroned him in Gandhi's hearts. . . . In him he found kindred spirit, a single minded seeker after truth, an aristocrat turned peasant and shoe maker in pursuit of the meaning of life who dedicated his wealth and talent and genius to the service of humanity, while he himself strove to the live by his body labour".

Tolstoy believed in the efficacy of manual labour for earning one's bread. He advocated performance of manual labour by everybody. He made a plea for manual labour in the interest of the poor and so also in the interest of the rich. His life was dedicated to the purpose of promoting the objective of an egalitarian society. His philosophy breathed in a large measure the message of extinguishment of socio-economic disparities, privileges, exploitation and creation of a society, whose cornerstones are equality, fraternity, fellowship, renunciation, non-exploitation and bread labour were enriched by Tolstoy's influence.

Gandhiji has unhesitatingly acknowledged his debt to the past. Hinduism, the oldest religion of India is well known for its non-violent and pacifist traditions. Its famous doctrine of *Advaita* and aphorisms like *Soham* and *Tat Tvam Asi* stand for spiritual immanence and emphasis the unity of all creations. It is true that there is no reference of non-violence in *Rigveda*, nevertheless, it affirms the doctrine of unity of all mankind. In the *Anusasan Parva* of the *Mahabharata*, Bhisma, while lying on death-bed, describes *Ahimsa* as the highest religion in his discourse to Yudhisthira.

Non-violence and peace are ancient beliefs in India. The excavations at Mohenjadaro and Harappa have revealed that the Indus Valley people were predominantly peace-loving. In fact, their pacifist attitude is considered to have been, partly responsible for the eventual extinction of their civilisation, which might have followed their defeat at the hands of the first wave of the more spirited and war like Aryans. In 1936, Gandhiji wrote, "There is no such thing as Gandhism. . . . I do not claim to have originated any new principle or doctrine. . . . I have nothing new to teach the world. Truth and non-violence are as old as the hills".

The Vaishnava ideal impressed Gandhiji very much. Narasingh Mehta, a saint poet of Gujarat described the Vaisnava ideal in the poem which formed part of the daily prayers at the Ashram. The poem reads as:

> A true Vaisnava is he who is moved by other's sufferings;
> Who helps people in distress, and feels no pride for having
>   done so.
> Respectful to everyone in the world, he speaks ill of none;
> Is self controlled in action, speech and thought
> Twice-blessed the mother who bore, such a one.
> He has an equal-seeing eye, and is free from all craving,
>   Another's wife is to him a mother;
> His tongue utters no untruth,
> And never his hand touches another's wealth.
> *Moha* and *Maya* have no power over him,
> In his mind reigns abiding detachment;
> He dances with a rapture to Rama's name—
> No centre of pilgrimage but is present in his person.
> A man he is without greed and cunning,
> And bulged of anger and desire;
> Offering reverence to such a one, says Narasingha,
> Will bring release to seventy-one generations of one's forbears.

Gandhiji said, "Narasingh, the best among the Vaisnavas, has given pride of place to non-violence". This means that a man who has no love in him is no Vaisnava. One who does not follow truth and has not acquired control over all his senses is not a Vaisnava. One does not become a Vaisnava simply by following the rituals. Non-violence in Vaisnava is not only concerned with human beings, but it also includes all living creatures.

Gandhiji had faith in Vaisnava Dharma, but he was least interested in attending the temples. He said, 'Being born in the Vaisnava faith, I had often to go to the Haveli. But it never appealed to me. I did not like its glitter and pomp. Also I heard rumours of immorality practised there, and lost all interest in it. Hence, I could gain nothing from the Haveli".

Gandhiji was influenced to a great extent by the *Light of Asia*. For the first time, he came in contact with Buddha's philosophy during his stay in England. He wrote,'The brothers (Theosophists) also recommended the *Light of Asia* by Sir Edwin Arnold, whom I knew till then as the author only of the Song Celestial, and I read it with even greater interest than I did the *Bhagvadgita*. Once I had begun it I could not leave off'. Buddha retained the ethical ideas of the orthodox religion, but repudiated the authority of the *Vedas* and the priests. He rejected rituals, caste system and sacrifice. He was much more interested in providing a remedy for the ills of life than in discussing metaphysical subtleties. His teaching was confined to the four Truths and eightfold path. The four Truths are —that there is suffering in the world, that there are causes of suffering, that there is cessation of suffering or a condition of *Nirvana*, and that there is a way to the realisation of *Nirvana*. The eight-fold path enunciated by Buddha as his first sermon at Sarnath for the realisation of *Nirvana* consist in right belief, right aim, right speech, right action, right living, right effort, right mindfulness, and right contemplation. The practice of these principles leads to *Nirvana*.

Buddha founded an ethical religion and Gandhiji adopts similar approach. Righteous living alone brings salvation. Gandhiji laid more emphasis on means than the ends because he feels that if pure means is rightly pursued and adopted, the desired goal can never be far off. He also prefer cosmic salvation and pains of births and re-births till the entire mankind are liberated. Gandhiji says, "Look at Gautama's compassion; said I. It was not confined to mankind, it was extended to all living beings. Does not one's heart overflow with love to think of the lamb joyously perched on his shoulders?" Gandhiji is opposed to segregation of man of one class from another as based on caste distinctions, sacraments, dogmas and rites. Buddha also demolished them and tried to evolve new social values in their place.

Non-violence is the essence of Buddhism. Buddha did not advocate a literal application of violence to the punishment of criminals and to war. Buddha teaches *Ahimsa* both as love and avoidance of injury to self and others. Positively *Ahimsa* finds expression in love, pity, tenderness and impartiality. The love that the Buddha teaches is the deliberately radiated well-wishing love towards all living things whatever. The Buddhist doctrine of violence is more practical and it steers clear of extremes. The path of the Buddha has been called the 'Middle way'.

The Buddha, although born as a man, is as Tathagata inconumerable, 'beyond all ways of telling'. He is the *Dhamma*, the Eternal law, the truth. The Buddha's teaching may be pointed out that the objective of the Bodhisattva in his search for Enlightenment was essentially ethical, that is, to put an end to suffering.

Buddhism takes a more realistic view of life. The Buddha was not content with the practice of good morals for reaching the ultimate goal of life. *Nirvana*, he said, was beyond good and evil, both of which bind the individual. He urged for the eradication of the notion of self; the individual must rise above name and aspect and he must see clearly the causal origination of all things and plunge into immortal. The Buddha's call of violence, according to the Metta Sutta is, "Let goodwill without measure prevail in the world, above, below, around, unstinted, unmixed with any feeling of differing or opposing interests. If a man remains steadfastly in this state of mind all the while he is awake, whether he be standing, walking, sitting or lying down, there is come to pass the sayings : Even in this world holiness has been found".

Buddhism laid considerable stress on non-violence, celibacy, non-possession and non-stealing. Buddha, by virtue of his strong moral sense, tried to achieve salvation. Gandhiji being a true disciple of Buddha, adopted and practised the same code of morality for achieving salvation.

Light of Asia not only preaches the spirit of renunciation of Buddha; it also preaches his philosophy of non-exploitation because Buddha's compassion for all living beings not only led him to be an advocate of non-injury, it also implies non-deprivation of anybody of his rightful dues. The philosophy of universal love, non-injury to living beings, sacrifice and renunciation for the sake of promoting the welfare of the universe and the principle of non-stealing as preached by Buddha and driven home to him through the *Light of Asia* had such deeper appeal for Gandhiji. The Buddhist compassion for suffering humanity, love for the entire universe, sacrifice and renunciation for the sake of the welfare of the entire creation and concern for the liberation of all from suffering and unhappiness drove home to Gandhiji the passion of serving the cause of humanity, a sense of sacrifice and renunciation for bettering their lot and a desire for service instead of exploitation. This passion and compassion stimulated his sense of non-exploitation and egalitarianism and prepared the foundation of his philosophy of *Sarvodaya.*

Jainism has its strong roots in Gujarat. The Jain traditions were very much in evidence in Gandhiji's Vaisnava family and his early acquaintance with Raichandbhai, a Jain devout, who emphasised the principle of austerities and the doctrine of suffering in religious life. Though Jainism stands as an opposition to Vedic orthodoxy, Gandhiji was deeply impressed by its philosophy of non-violence and righteousness.

The founder of Jainism, Mahavir, was born in 547 B.C. He rejects Vedic sacrifices and the texts and enjoin them but he retains morals of the *Upanishads*. According to Jainism the way to *Nirvana* is a three-fold path. It consists of right faith, right knowledge, and right conduct. These three are called the *ratnatraya*, the three jewels of *Dharma*. The right conduct consists of the observance of non-violence, truthfulness, non-stealing, chastity, and non-attachment to worldly things. Jainism stretches the practice of non-violence to such an extremity as to forbid one to take the life of even an insect. This extreme form of non-violence, Gandhiji felt was not workable for the ordinary run of mankind; he therefore, spoke of relative non-violence; the concrete situation afford the criterion of judgement for the subtle application of non-violence as an accepted principle.

In the *Ayaravgasuta* a Jain text dating probably from third or fourth century B.C. *Ahimsa* is preached in the following words:

> "All saints and lords in the past, in the present and in the future, they all say thus, speak thus, announce thus and declare

thus : one may not kill, nor ill-use, nor insult, nor torment, nor prosecute any kind of living being, any kind of creature, any kind of thing having a soul, any kind of being."

The Jain poet Hemachandra praised non-killing in the following verses:

> "*Ahimsa* is like a loving mother of all beings, *Ahimsa* is like a stream of nectar in the desert *Samsara*, *Ahimsa* is a course of rain-clouds to the forest fire of sufferings. The best herb of healing for the beings that are tormented by the disease, called the perpetual return of existence is *Ahimsa*."

Gandhiji refuses to identify his *Ahimsa* with mere mechanical non-killing. To him, the extreme application of non-violence by the Jains is based on the misleading assumption that the pain and suffering of death are more terrible than that of life. The Jains distort meaning of *Ahimsa* by emphasising the sacredness of sub-human life. Gandhiji, on the other hand, is not altogether opposed to the killing of snakes, monkeys, mosquitoes and small insects, if they cannot, otherwise, be put out of harm's way.

The Jainas believe that the entire world is literally packed with an infinite number of embodied souls, their bodies being either gross and visible or subtle and invisible. All the elements are animated with souls. The embodiment of the spirit in the material body is the cause of misery. So life means pain even to souls with invisible bodies. To become a *muktatma*, a soul liberated from the bonds of the body, the individual must complete the process of *nirjara*. Jainism has been an important factor in sustaining and deepening the tradition of non-violence in India.

Jainism had been a greater living force in Gujarat than in any other part of India. Gandhiji read with great interest not only the life of Mahavir and the ethical teachings of the Jainas but also *Saddarsana Samuccya*, the philosophical texts of Haribhadra Suri. Jainsim laid great stress on non-violence, celibacy, non-possession and non-stealing. Gandhiji's family contact with the Jains and the Jain philosophy of non-violence accentuated his ethical outlook in favour of communitarianism. Jainism as a religious faith arose as an offshoot in Hinduism, as an attempt at reforming Hinduism in order to make it less violent and more humane, compassionate and a selfless faith, infusing a greater sense of sociability into the doctrine. The Jain philosophy no doubt is primarily a philosophy of non-injury to living beings and a philosophy of non-violence; but positively speaking, it is a religion that preaches compassion not only for man but for all living beings.

The Vaisnavic family influence of self-sacrifice, self-surrender, identification with God's creation and renunciation of worldly possessions, on Gandhiji, had its manifestation in form of compassion for the suffering humanity, and egalitarian philosophy.

Islam is a religion of peace and brotherhood. The very word 'Islam' means peace, safety or salvation. The Prophet himself was extremely gentle, humane and more modest than a virgin in her veil. To his disciples, he was always indulgent, he rebuked none. However, the *Koran* favours war against the aggressor. The Prophet himself waged defensive wars, although at the end forgave his defeated enemies. Yet, the Prophet preferred non-violence to violence.

Islam has become associated in the common mind with violence and coercion. But, Gandhiji regards Islam as a religion of peace in the same sense in which Christianity, Buddhism and Hinduism are. The followers of Islam have occasionally been too free with the sword, but that is not in terms of the *Koran*, but the environment in which Islam was born. According to Gandhiji, the chief contribution of Islam has been the brotherhood of man. The message of Prophet was essentially a message of kindness and consideration, peace and love, non-violence as a means of conquering evil than violence. Nevertheless *Koran* permits defensive war and war against the wrongdoer.

Islam basically does not provide for forcible conversion. Prophet said, "Let there be no compulsion in religion, the right way is in itself distinct from the wrong". The Muslim salutation as *Salam Alaikum* means 'live in peace and prosperity'. Islam also preaches religious toleration and universal brotherhood. Gandhiji, likely, strive for the Hindu-Muslim unity during his political career and urged for toleration and due respect towards all faiths to maintain the communal harmony.

Islam played an important role in shaping Gandhiji's views in regard to religion. He very often quoted passages from *Koran* in his prayer meetings. In South Africa, he studied Islam under the influence of some Muslim friends. His friend, Seth Abdulla was well versed in Islamic literature. He said: "Contact with him gave me a fair amount of practical knowledge of Islam. When we came closer to each other, we had long discussions on religious topics". A friend recommended Carlyle's *Heroes and Hero-worship*. He read the chapter on the Hero as a prophet and learnt of the prophet's greatness and bravery and austere living. He also studied Washington Irving's *Life of Mahomed and His Successors*, and said these books raised Mahomed in his estimation. He also purchased Sale's translation of the *Koran* and read it with great interest.

Gandhiji read the *Bible* during his studies in England and the *New Testament* impressed him very much, especially the *Sermon on the Mount*. He visited churches and participated in their religious performances. His deep interest and passionate devotion to Christianity made him realise its truths. If any religion other than Hinduism had touched and pervaded the very being of Gandhiji, it was Christianity. He said, "I have not been able to see any difference between the *Sermon on the Mount* and the *Bhagvadgita*. What the *Sermon* describes in a graphic manner, the *Bhagvadgita* reduces to a scientific formula. It may not be a scientific book in the accepted sense of the term, but it has argued out the law of love—the law of abandon as I call it—in a scientific manner. The *Sermon on the Mount* gives the same law in wonderful language. Today, supposing, I was deprived of the *Gita* and forget all its contents but had a copy of the *Sermons*, I should derive the same joy from it as I do from the *Gita*".

Christianity has got its origin in Judaism as Jesus pronounced, his doctrine was nothing but the teaching of the Old Testament Prophets, i.e., the law of love. Jesus, however, makes the law revolutionary and transforming by raising it from the level of reciprocity to that of non-retaliation and creative purpose. Christ and his teachings occupy a unique place in the history of non-violence and pacifism. Gandhiji said, "Christianity's peculiar contribution is that of active love. No other religion says so firmly that God is love. . . . Christians, however, as a whole have denied the principles with their wars". Some incidents, recorded in the Gospels show that Jesus asked the physical force. But, there are numerous instances where the Jesus condemned the use of physical force and preached the principle of love. His life is the story of intense suffering for the love of humanity.

The entire teaching of the Christ logically follows from his conception of the universal, loving fatherhood of God, and brotherhood of man. Jesus quotes two commandments of the *Old Testament*, saying 'Thou shall love thy God', and 'Thou shall love thy neighbour as thyself'. The two commandments, says Jesus, are like one another and on them hang all the law and the prophets. Jesus was for the Kingdom of Heaven. He preached this revolutionary doctrine and was of the opinion that Jesus should give up violence and convert enemies into friends through his technique of love. Similarly Gandhiji also strove for the stateless and non-violent society.

The life and character of Gandhiji is similar to that of Christ. Gandhiji's ethics is restricted to his own sect or religion. He is immoral and irreligious towards men of other religious faiths. He endeavours to save Hinduism from falling to such degrading condition. He resorted to fast unto death for the removal of untouchability. The Cross is the symbol of sacrifice and *satyagraha* is the crown of it. *Satyagraha* is the working principle in spirit. The spirit of Cross is progressively manifest from the picketing of foreign clothes and campaign against salt tax to the self imposed fast till death. To quote S.K. George, "For fasting unto death in obedience to an inner conviction is, Gandhi himself says, only the final form, the crown of *Satyagraha*, from the picketing of a foreign cloth shop to the starving of oneself to death. The Cross of Christ can yet be a working principle of conquering love and overcoming evil everywhere".

Gandhiji wondered at Christ's non-violent character and his faith in non-violence was confirmed. This is the reason that he called Jesus, 'he prince of *Satyagrahis*'. Christ's simple life, austere living and highly moral teaching were the most inspiring factors among the Western thinkers of truth and non-violence. In London, he renewed his study of the *Bible* especially the positive aspect of the Christianity. He said, "Jesus played a great part in my life unconsciously how much, I do not know, consciously how much, I do not know. When I began to read the *Sermon on the Mount* I felt the beauty of it. I cannot say that it is singular, or that it is not to be found in other religions. But the presentation is unique. . . . So many of my words are chosen from the *Bible*. In my takes I cannot avoid reference to *Bible*. I am unable to speak without referring to it". It has been said that Gandhiji embarrassed Christ but rejected Christianity.

Although Gandhiji did not identify himself with orthodox Christianity, the message of the *Bible*, the *New Testament* and the *Sermon on the Mount* had shaken the vital fiber in him. E. Stanley said, "Mahatma Gandhi was a Hindu—a deeply Christianised Hindu, more Christianised than most Christians". To quote Kingsley Martin, "I regard Gandhi as probably being of all modern leaders the most faithful interpreter of the philosophy of the Gospels". Thus it amply proved that Gandhiji lived the life of a devout Christian.

Jesus was primarily concerned with the creation of a better world, where love, fellowship, and fraternity shall prevail. Regarding Jesus, Gandhiji said, 'He was certainly the highest example of one who wished to give everything asking nothing in return· and not caring what creed might happen to be professed by the recipient'. The spirit of love for and service to all, and non-acquisitiveness and renunciation preached by Jesus, must have helped Gandhiji to properly understand equality, fraternity and fellowship. To quote Joseph J. Doke,

> "Naturally his imagination is profoundly stirred by the *Sermon on the Mount* and the idea of the self-renunciation pictured there as well as in the *Bhagvadgita* and the *Light of Asia* with his complete assent. Self-mastery, self-denial and self-surrender, under the guidance of the spirit of God, are in his conception of life, stepping stones to the ultimate goal of all—the goal of Buddha, the goal as he interprets it, of John the Evangelist—absolute absorption of redeemed Man in God."

The *New Testament* not only emphasises on work or efforts of the individual for one's existence and prosperity; it lays equal stress on bodily labour, since sacrifice of body for the sake of real development of the individual forms the core of such emphasis. The sacrifice of the body does not mean committing suicide but sacrifice of bodily efforts, or luxuries, laziness, idleness or pampering of the body. It implies labour with the body, sacrifice of bodily comfort that arises as a corollary of idleness and enjoyment of real worth of life, the intellectual excellences and spiritual bliss by way of work. Jesus did not claim freedom from work for his own sustenance.

It was in 1889 Gandhiji came across two Theosophists brother. They talked to him about the *Gita*. They were reading Sir Edwin

Arnold's ranslation of *Gita—The Song Celestial*—and they invited him to read the original with them. The very first reading of it made a deep impression on him. The *Gita* constitutes the quintessence of the doctrine of *dharma*. It was to Gandhiji the unfailing guide in all circumstances. He said, "When doubt haunts me, when disappointments stare me in the face, and when I see not one ray of light on the horizon, I turn to the *Bhagvadgita*, and find a verse to comfort me; and I immediately begin to smile in the midst of overwhelming sorrow. My life has been full of external tragedies, and if they have not left any visible and indelible effect on me, I owe it to the teachings of the *Bhagvadgita*."

Gita is the most revered scripture for Gandhiji. He said, "The impression has ever since been growing on me with the result that I regard it today as the book par excellence for the knowledge of Truth". The *Gita* exhorts men to fight like a *Karmayogi*. The great sages fight in all ages in the spirit of detachment and surrender to God. Renunciation in action is the message of the *Gita*. Gandhiji said, "But after forty years unremitting endeavour fully to enforce the teaching of the *Gita* in my own life, I have, in all humility, felt that perfect renunciation is impossible without perfect observance of *ahimsa* in every shape and form". For Gandhiji, *Gita* is a book of spiritual reference. He learnt from the *Gita* that religion is not opposed to material good. It is a misconception to hold that in business, vocation and day-to-day work, religion has no place and that religion is only for attaining spiritual salvation. The *Gita* dispels all such erroneous views.

The *Gita* inspires us to do our duties, neglecting the suffering and torture that we receive in course of our action. Again, renunciation of reward does not mean that we should ignore the result or remain ignorant of it. Everyone must know the effect of his actions, his capacity for doing a particular work and the means that he employs. But one should not be engrossed too much over his success. He should curb his passions and develop a sense of renunciation towards worldly ambitions and gains. To quote Gandhiji,

> "This is the unmistakable teaching of the *Gita*. He who gives up action falls. He who gives up only the reward rises. But renunciation of fruit in no way means indifference to the result. In regard to every action one must know the result that is

expected to follow, the means thereto, and the capacity for it. He, who, being thus equipped, is without desire for the result and is yet wholly engrossed in the due fulfilment of the task before him is said to have renounced the fruits of his action".

Louis Fischer remarked, "There are devout Hindus, and mystic Hindus, who sit and meditate and fast and go naked and live in the Himalayan caves. But Gandhi aimed to be ever active, ever useful and ever needless. This was the realisation he craved. Like everybody else, Gandhi had attachment. He sought to slough them off'. God-realisation is possible only through righteous action. The devotion to God must accompany living service to humanity. Mere telling of beads would not achieve anything for us. If the devotee refrains from action and does not wage war for establishing a righteous and spiritual universe, there can be no salvation for him. The *Gita* says, "No one attained his goal without action. Even men like Janaka attained salvation through action. If even I were lazily to cease working, the world would perish. How much more necessary, then, for the people at large to engage in action ?" A seeker after Truth realises God through ceaseless performance of actions done in the detachment of spirit. One who acts in the spirit of sacrifice with utmost selflessness realises God.

The teachings of the *Gita*, especially the verses 62 and 63 of chapter 2, impressed him most and the book proved for him to be of priceless worth. Gandhiji wrote, "The verses in the second chapter made a deep impression on my mind and they still ring in my ears. The book struck me as one of priceless worth. The impression has ever since been growing on me with the result that I regard it today as the book par excellence for the knowledge of Truth. It has afforded me invaluable help in my moments of gloom". Sri Mahadev Desai held the view that every moment of Gandhiji's life is a conscious effort to live the message of the *Gita*. No other book influenced him so deeply as the study of the *Gita*. He learnt a good deal about *aparigraha* and *sambhava* from this book only. The teachings of the *Gita* became an infallible guide of conduct to him.

Religion was an aid to Gandhiji in this endeavour. It gave him a technique of life and a method of investigation. Gandhiji, however, wanted to bring the technique into action. He considered *Gita* as his spiritual dictionary where he found solution for his problems at the most crucial moments of his life. *Gita* was born to lift Arjuna from his despondency and the teaching given to Arjuna was the teaching given to all mankind. The *Gita* ideal of the 'Sthitaprajna' gripped his imagination. He became fond of it and made its recital part of his daily prayer. Similarly, the portrayal of the 'Bhakta' in the *Gita* inspired him. The Bhakta's qualities of friendliness, meekness, compassion, unperturbable and contentment fascinated him. The *Gita* teaches the cultivation of *Samatva* and the means of doing so is *Bhakti* accompanied with *Jyana*, i.e. service of every living creature without thought of reward. And the cultivation of *Bhakti* helps one to attain self-realisation. Gandhiji derived from *Gita* an equal regard to all.

The secret of the *Gita* which Gandhiji discovered and deduced into a commentary on the *Gita—Anasakti Yoga. Anasakti* means the cultivation of the habit of doing one's duty with zeal and efficiency remaining of the same time indifferent to its utility to oneslf. Gandhiji pointed out that renunciation of fruit in no way means indifference to the reuslt. He has treated *Gita* as a work on religion, ethics and philosophy all combined into one. Here religion is *Karmayoga*, ethics is *Anasakti* and *Bhakti* and philosophy is *Jnana* as also self-realisation after absolute submission of the self to God. The whole stress of *Gita* is for strictly following the *Karma* or Karmayoga and Gandhiji lays greater stress on *Anasaktiyoga* of *Gita* for self-realisation which is eternal peace. To Gandhiji, *Jnana* and *Bhakti* are both subsidiary to *Karma* and all the three are subsidiary to *Anasakti*. And *Bhakta*, *Jnani, Karmayogi, Sthitaprajna, Trigunatita*, all are more or less one, almost identical and all perform actions constantly in a spirit of detachment. And once a man cultivates this spirit of detachment, Truth and *Ahimsa* lead him to self-realisation. He agreed that *Gita* do not preach the doctrine of *Ahimsa*, but it is an earlier doctrine that the *Gita* takes for granted.

Gandhiji believed that the *Mahabharata*, the war in the *Gita* symbolise the battle-ground between good and evil in human nature. He further stressed that the human heart is the battle-field on which a constant war is going on between these good and evil forces. Kurushetra was to him the *Dharmakshetra*, the field of battle in the heart of man. He believed in an incarnation of God who has performed extraordinary service to mankind. The theory of *Avatara* symbolises man's constant effort and struggle to become like unto God. He realised that the *Gita* is a scripture not only for the Hindus but for humanity at large. It teaches us to regard others as oneself and the spirit of liberalism to understand others faith. *Gita* convincingly argued that *Samanvaya* for reaching the Truth. Every body without hindrance has to follow his own path. Universal soul in which all the souls exist is God and true end of human effort consist in knowing that universal soul which is the one source of all.

Throughout Gandhiji's life, the *Gita* remained the source of his pleasure and joy, solace and strength, and the reference book for resolving all knotty problems both in private and public life. To quote Gandhiji, "Today the *Gita* is not only my *Bible*, or my *Kuran*; it is more than that—it is my mother. . . . She has never changed, she has never failed me. When I am in difficulty or distress, I seek refuge in her bosom". Later on, he said that the *Gita* had been his *Kamadhenu*, his guide, his open sesame on hundreds of moments of doubt and difficulty. He cannot recall a single occasion when it has failed him.

Gita provides the apparatus for reaching the destination of Divine life. For the attainment of Divine Self that is the highest ambition of man and the ultimate objective of the creation, the individual must be liberated from the clutches of the ego. But the liberation according to the *Gita* consists in the transcendence of self-compassion for the whole world and service to the entire creation. Dr. Radhakrishnan remarked, "The liberated souls take upon themselves the burden of the redemption of the whole world. Anchored in the timeless foundation of our spiritual existence, the freed soul, the eternal individual, works for the *Jivalok*. While possessing the individuality of body, life and mind, he yet retains the universality of spirit". The message of the *Gita* is one of attainment of Divinity in human life and equivalence with God by way of transcendence of the ego, sublimation of the self and service of the whole world.

The technique of renunciation that forms the cornerstone of the message of self-realisation as preached by the *Gita* profoundly influenced Gandhiji, and it converted him inch by inch to the doctrine of egalitarianism. He derived inspiration for his thought from the philosophy of self-realisation, complete identification with the community, renunciation for the sake of the community, and welfare of all preached in the *Gita*. His idea of *Sarvodaya* also derived its primary inspiration from the *Gita*. The idea of Bread Labour equally derived its inspiration from the *Karmayoga* of the

Gita inspired him. His idea of Trusteeship of the rich can be traced to the philosophy of renunciation of the fruits of one's action for the community as advocated in the *Gita*. Thus, the *Gita* proved to be a decisive factor in shaping his philosophy in the right direction.

Gandhiji was also influenced by *Manusmrti*. He learnt form it that truth underlies morality. It revealed him that moral life is essentially valuable. Gandhiji said,

> "But the fact that I had learnt to be tolerant to other religions did not mean that I had any living faith in God. I happened about this time to come across *Manusmrti* which was amongst my father's collection. The story of the creation and similar things did not impress me very much, but on the contrary made me incline somewhat towards atheism. But one thing took deep root in me—the conviction that morality is the basis of things, and that truth is the substance of all morality. Truth became my sole objective. It began to grow in magnitude everyday, my definition of it also has been ever widening."

Gandhiji was also influenced by the *Upanishads*. The *Upanishads* gave us first the message of non-violence. The Chhandogya declared that non-violence was an ethical quality of man. Patanjali held out non-violence as one of the five cardinal disciplines of man's life; he did not believe that it was merely a negative doctrine of avoidance of violence but stressed that it manifested good will towards all.

Hindu ethics since the time of the *Upanishads* had always laid stress on the virtue of *ahimsa* to all living beings, human or otherwise. According to Rhys Davids, *ahimsa* is expressly mentioned for the first time in the *Chhandogya Upanishad* "where five ethical qualities, one being *ahimsa*, are said to be equivalent to a part of sacrifice of which the whole life of man is made an epitome". The *Gita* is the quintessence of the *Upanishads*.

Ramayana left an indelible impression on Gandhiji's spiritual thought. He went through the sacred book, *Ramayana*. The influence of the *Ramayana* of Tulsidas in Gandhi is next to that of the *Gita*. He said, "What, however, left a deep impression on me was the reading of the *Ramayana* before my father. During part of his illness my father was in Porbander. There every evening he used to listen to the *Ramayana*. The reader was a great devotee of Rama. He had a melodious voice. . . . I must have been thirteen at that time, but

I quite remember being enraptured by his reading. That laid the foundation of my deep devotion to the *Ramayana*".

Gandhiji was also influenced by *Mahabharata*. He learnt very much from it. To quote Dr. Radhakrishnan, "The great epic of *Mahabharata* exposes the futility of war by pointing out that the victory of the Pandavas was but a mockery, as only seven persons survived out of the millions who were engaged in that colossal conflict". Gandhiji said, "I have maintained in the teeth of orthodox Hindu opposition that the *Mahabharata* is a book written to establish the futility of war and violence". This shows that war and violence can come to an end only through non-violence and peace. Insistence on war and violence brings to an end all peace and tranquillity. So, Gandhiji adopted non-violence as the key to the solution of all the problems of life. The reading of *Mahabharat* book confirmed his faith in truth and non-violence.

Ramayana and *Mahabharata* beckon us to practice non-violence for our civilised existence. *Ramayana* portrays the magnificence of morality. The message of *Mahabharata* is no less certain about it. Vyasa, concluding his great epic, cries with uplifted hands : "Wealth and pleasure accrue to men through morality. Why do men follow this truth". It proclaims that war annihilates all. Bhisma extols non-violence as the highest religion and the highest penance; it is also the highest truth from which all duty proceeds. Kapila extols non-violence as one of the sure ways to attain divine knowledge. Gandhiji wanted to spiritualise politics. In so doing, he was merely rehearsing the ancient Indian dream which he found in *Ramayana*.

Gandhiji was influenced by Harischandra's story. After getting permission from his father, he once witnessed a play on Satyavadi Harischandra which captivated him. He remarked that Harischandra captured his heart. He said, "Why should not all be truthful like Harischandra was the question I asked myself day and night. To follow truth and to go through all the ordeals Harischandra went through was the one ideal it inspired in me". His religion was impressed by Harischandra's story. Like Harischandra, he also suffered for preaching and practising truthfulness.

Gandhiji was also deeply influenced by the story of Shravana's devotion to his parents. He read the play Shravana Pitribhakti with intense interest which left an indelible impression on his mind. He learnt the lesson of selfless service and devotion from the pictures depicting Shravana carrying, by means of slings fitted for his shoulders, his blind parents on pilgrimage. Shravana became his model.

3

ON LEADERSHIP

Gandhiji proclaimed two basic ideals as keys to this future, truth and freedom, that is, as he himself interpreted them. Liberation from the yoke of foreign rule, which, as a member of the educated class of the new India, he adopted a self-evident goal, seemed to him to be the primary prerequisite for relieving the dreadful misery endured by the Indian masses. He believed that it was British rule, British self-interest and British power politics which were responsible for this misery. It may be said that it was his sympathy for the suffering mass of the people which drove him into politics and made him the liberator of India. In this view an Independent India either had to provide above all for the freedom of the very poorest people or it seemed to him to be worthless. His concept of truth corresponded to this deeply rooted and fundamental feeling for humanity. By truth, he meant the re-establishment of those human relationships that God approved of, and this required the active cooperation of all those who regarded themselves as good in God's eyes, in a common effort to create for all men a properly human existence. To this extent he was able to term himself a practical idealist. This also meant, however that truth had to adopt itself to the varying conditions of life and hence that it was a factor capable of change in the constant flux of things.

Gandhiji knew that he had constantly to investigate and to search if he was to arrive at the truth in any particular situation, that a seeker after truth always had a experiment, and that his unchanging goal could only be pursed by listening carefully to his inner voice. Both freedom and truth stemmed for him from his religion, from that profound faith from which he drew the remarkable strength that the trails of his life necessitated; yet it was a religion that admitted on dogma. Thus, although he was an orthodox Hindu, he was open-minded and tolerant. It was this religiosity which made him the spiritual leader of the nation, the prophet of a new age, and won him the honorary title of Mahatma, a great spirit who responded to everything human and to the distress of all men.

As the fundamental method for achieving his goals he advocated non-violence, *Ahimsa*—a principle which, in itself, forms no essential part of the Hindu religion. Gandhiji, whose family had maintained close friendships with the Jains, had absorbed the Jaina conception of life in early childhood and he was glad to find this corroborated when a Christian missionary in Africa pointed out to him the passage in Mathew (5.39) where Jesus also commanded that one should not resist evil with violence. When he found these ideas treated at length in Tolstoy too, he constantly made use of them to base his own teachings on Christian evidence, so that he could call on Christians to adopt them.

Upto the end Gandhiji adhered to his principle, although in practice he often allowed exceptions, as, for example, in 1947 when he accepted the use of weapons to protect those that were threatened in the Calcutta disturbances, or when he declared that violence was permissible for the attainment of a morally laudable goal. The question whether *Ahimsa* should also apply to the army and to the police was first raised in the Congress in 1940, when a Japanese attack of India was expected; non-violence was never declared as a binding article of faith for the individual members of Congress, not even for Gandhiji's closest associates like Nehru, who often spoke out against it.

At first Gandhiji was convinced that his method would result in certain success and he always adhered to the view that it was the most effective way for the weak and suffering to improve their situation. On the other hand, he frequently admitted that its chances of success were only fifty-fifty.

The method of non-violence was first adopted by the Liberation Movement and the Congress for the campaigns between 1919 and 1922. It was suitable, firstly because the Indians as a people without arms had no other way of revolting, and secondly because the remarkable response that it found among the masses promised a successful expansion of the struggle for the liberation. And in any case the Liberation Movement had already subscribed to this principle, previously. What had been done before Gandhiji's time to shake off the British yoke, had been confined to debates and resolutions, or in other words to measures, which were of an entirely constitutional nature. The politician in whom Gandhiji found his first model, was Gokhale, one of the strictest and noblest representatives of this purely constitutional approach. The new element introduced by Gandhiji was that other, far more radical though non-violent, actions should be accepted and put into practice. He rapidly intensified his programme by calling for mass demonstrations on a grand scale, for systematic non-cooperation in state and public functions and finally for open civil disobedience, though only in the mild form of breaking the salt tax law. This was also included in the new programme of passive resistance against a government which opposed the truth. Legal notices were not discussed in the great stir which Gandhiji's watchwords immediately aroused.

The political task that Gandhiji set himself admittedly continued the already existent Liberation Movement but differed from it in one important point. Both wanted liberation from British domination, both wanted an Independent India; but Gandhiji's precursors, who were primarily men from the upper middle class with a European educational background, only referred to liberation on the international level. In as far as they considered problems on the home front at all, they wanted to postpone their solution until the British had left, in the belief that everything would sort itself out later. The only form of liberation that Gandhiji regarded as worthwhile was one which would release all Indians from a state of dependence and misery.

The older generation could speak of a 'national movement' by introducing the western concept of a 'nation', whereas Gandhiji immediately saw that no Indian 'nation' as such yet existed, and that to the masses that were close to his heart it did not seem to make sense. He realised that at best a nation could only arise during and after the experience of liberation, for the only feeling of solidarity which Indians could conceive of at that time which transcended the regional caste divisions was at the most a sense of belonging to one of the peoples that had grown together through sharing a common language and history, often under the rule of a single local dynasty. Around 1900 one could perhaps already speak of Bengali or Marathi peoples, but certainly not of an 'Indian' nation. Gandhiji kept this in mind when, in 1915, he returned to his home land after an absence of 22 years in South Africa, and decided after some years of initial political experiments to join the great political movement.

Gandhiji first created an entirely new concept, that of *Satyagraha*, the 'way to inner truth', which was to lead to freedom. By this means he could appeal equally to all Indians no matter to what people, religion or caste they belonged. Furthermore, it also gave him the tactical opportunity for putting into practice what he considered should be the 'truth' in any given situation. Even the simplest of Indians immediately grasped that British rule was 'non-truth', as it obviously failed to fulfil the duties that the religions and holy traditions, both in Hinduism and in Islam, assigned to a government.

The observer can add in retrospect at this point that the British allowed far more spiritual freedom than, say the Moslem governments. Precisely their religious indifference created the spiritual climate in which both the earlier spiritual regeneration and then the Gandhi Movement were able to evolve. But as the British were simply foreigners to the broad mass of Indians, they could not make use of this fact. Moreover they were the first to create a constitutional state which provided the legal opportunities for Gandhiji's large-scale demonstrations and provocative publicity campaigns. And by keeping to these rules and by only acting when existent laws were actually violated, they gave Gandhiji's movement a far greater scope than some states, less concerned with their reputation for being 'Constitutional', would tolerate today. So Gandhiji was able to advance in a sphere that his forerunners had been so far from utilising to the same extent, and was able to term 'Constitutional' actions which the older Congressmen did not dare to undertake. The combination of *satyagraha* and *ahimsa* worked like a magic spell on the Indian masses and their success confirmed Gandhiji's speculation.

Admittedly Gandhiji knew the dangers that his new course involved. He demanded of his *satyagrahis* a degree of self-discipline and spiritual preparation that no one had previously called for. In his public projects he only tolerated participants who had proved that they could set to work independently, who were fully aware of their moral responsibility, and who were prepared as genuine disciples of *ahimsa* patiently and steadfastly to endure all the violence to which their opponents would subject them. During the period preparatory to his first mass campaign Gandhiji had trained in his *ashram* a small elite on which he could rely, and had then set up small cells for similar purposes in many other parts. But his inner sense of responsibility was too great to overlook any symptom that augured ill.

It was this excessive caution that brought about his first political set back; he called off the movement that was prepared for February 1922 shortly before it was due to begin, because some peasants at a village in the Ganges valley (Chauri Chaura), who were not in the least connected with him, had attacked a police station and burnt some Indian Policemen to death. Today it is plain to see that this campaign, which was to begin in Bardoli, would have set the whole of India aflame. As even the local representatives of the Congress had come out on the side of the mobs on this occasion and thus openly violated Gandhiji's principles, he thought he could foresee similar developments occurring elsewhere, and so retracted his call for the struggle to begin. He certainly abandoned a great opportunity at this time, but he did so to prevent his moral principles from being endangered.

The duty of every *satyagrahi* was to adhere so persistently to his own convictions that he would finally force them upon his dissenting opponents. Gandhiji, who had, of course, been arrested immediately after calling of the movement, now realised that his most vital task was to impress this duty on his followers still more deeply before initiating a new campaign. He extended the scope of his actions from mere demonstration, processions and proclamations to the systematic refusal of broad masses of the people to cooperate in any way with the organs of the British administration in schools, courtrooms and local government, etc. This non-violent, non-cooperation dominated Gandhiji's next campaign and provided the classic formulation of his method. A boycott of this kind had first been employed by the Bengalis in 1905 when they opposed the dismemberment of their country by Lord Curzon. It had been successful. Gandhiji now proclaimed the boycott over the whole of India and started a mass movement of size which no one had previously dreamt of.

The decisive turning-point was that Gandhiji not only declared himself to be concerned above all with the welfare of the masses but that he conveyed this message to them so poignantly that they were actually inspired by it. The broad mass of the Indian people, which had played no active part in politics for centuries, was so aroused by this leader that it joined in the resistance movement.

During his numerous journeys and meetings Gandhiji usually

spoke only of matters that moved the ordinary man. He advised them to cooperate more effectively and actively at home and in the village in order to gradually mitigate their own distress. He asked of them only what they could all do; to set to work, to spin to ignore the British administration and to join the mass meetings that were organised. He declared that they no longer needed to fear the ruling class because, if they all stood together, they were strong enough to have their own hands. As these words came from a man whom they instinctively trusted and whom they immediately felt to be one of themselves, the response was unbelievably great.

Such ideas could also be directed against the social and economic order which had existed before the advent of the British and had established itself under their strictly 'Capitalistic' economy. The Congress, in particular, had many members who belonged to this layer of society and whose political aims in no way included a revolutionary incitement of the masses of this kind. Gandhiji had admittedly started to work with the Congress simply because it constituted the only All-India organisation, but he soon realised that there was a chasm between the majority in the Congress and himself, a chasm which was later to grow still wider. For when the British, under the imminent pressure of the growing mass movements, introduced constitutional reforms and first consulted and then allowed the Indian politicians responsible participation in the current affairs of state, the men of practical politics, to whom Gandhiji's ideas had seemed vague and risky from the start, found a way of working for the liberation of India from within the new parliaments and ministerial posts vacated for them far more convenient to them than Gandhiji with his watchwords—self-discipline, asceticism, popular appeal and uprisings.

Admittedly Gandhiji breathed new life into the Congress and it was due to him that it developed from a refined debating club to a truly popular mass organisation. Many of the elected representatives and parliamentarians, however, where by no means genuine 'Gandhians', not even Nehru. Gandhiji consciously reckoned with this. He was fond, in any case, of creating special organisations for new projects, though he could no more do without the cooperation of the Congress, then the Congress could do without him. Both required the other and despite their differences of opinion they were compelled time and again to accept a course of compromise. This meant in practical terms that Gandhiji tried to exploit the Congress, and the Congress him, both tolerating a great deal provided that their common cause was furthered. For this reason, Gandhiji, to whom state, parliamentary and even administrative work were alien, soon started playing with the idea of withdrawing from everyday politics.

Gandhiji wanted to hand over the leadership of the struggle to a man of practice, C.R. Das, the most important Bengali leader. The latter, however, died soon afterwards. In 1934, Gandhiji formally resigned from the Congress. Admittedly his reputation among the people was so great that nothing could occur without his approval, and at times of crisis or before new large scale actions he was continually given powers that practically made him a dictator, as, for example, in the 'Quit India' campaign, the last mass uprising, the turbulent outcome of which cannot be imputed to him personally since the British made the mistake of arresting him on the first morning. But the nearer the hour of freedom came, the more he consciously stepped into the background, leaving the leadership to the politicians and above all to the most capable of the younger generation, Nehru. He was aware that Nehru's views differed from his own in certain essential points but saw at the same time that it was to him that the British would hand over power at the decisive moment.

Just as Nehru was always incorrigibly suspicious of anyone who earned money, Gandhiji was prejudiced against the 'educated upper class' of his people. He reproached them with thanking their comfortable life and higher education to 'violence', since these things could only be paid for by exploiting the mass of the poor. In his view they should 'do penitence' for it by working personally for the mitigation of the peoples' distress and by contributing their own fortune to this end, in accordance with his own example in his *ashram*. Even a welfare state for all, whose beneficiaries, however, stayed at home instead of working in the village or helping in some other way, would not have been to Gandhiji's liking. The middle class should go out to those places where real misery was crying out for help, an idea that Gandhiji's teacher Gokhale had wonted to realise in the 'Society of India's Servants'. Thus, when the politicians spoke of the national 'unity' which had to be created as a precondition for liberation, they were mostly thinking only of the politically conscious layer of society, whereas Gandhiji really wanted to include everyone: the poorest and the outcasts and even those who were conscious outsiders. It was in serving this task that he expended his greatest powers—in winning over the 'Pariahs' and in the enlistment of the Muslims to the cause.

The Pariahs or untouchables—Gandhiji called them *Harijans* or children of God, just as here in the Middle Ages those suffering from the plague were called 'good people'—were below the lowest of all the castes in the Hindu social hierarchy. At that time they numbered 35 millions and to endure, in addition to their material distress, the social stigma of untouchability. Gandhiji's humanitarian feeling and sense of justice had discovered this ulcer in the Indian body politic early. He was determined that any 'liberation' of India had to include the release of this group too. The problem became politically acute when, in their attempt to create as many minorities as possible, the British wished to reserve special parliamentary seats for them and thus make them an element capable of separate action. This problem became still more extreme when the Muslim League seized the opportunity to attract this minority to its own cause, in the attempt to deprive the Hindus of their support and so considerably to reduce the Hindu majority, for this would have weakened the position of the latter and strengthened that of their opponents in the votes and division of seats that were planned for the parliaments. Jinnah even went so far in the first Indian Cabinet as to award one of the places allowed to the Muslims to an untouchable, thus openly playing off this group against the Hindu majority in the very heart of the central government.

Thus humanitarian and political motives combined to intensify Gandhiji's resistance; he even proclaimed a fast to the point of death if this regulation came into force. He achieved a reasonable settlement, which the government of Republican India had striven hard to put into effect in so far as is legislatively possible. But it is a noteworthy symptom of how great the calamitous differences created by the old Indian tradition were, that the leader of the untouchables, Dr. Ambedkar, was not among the politicians who fully trusted Gandhiji.

Gandhiji's efforts to win over the Muslims, who, numbering some 60 millions at that time, formed the largest and politically most significant minority, were less successful. A timely settlement with his powerful group was, of course, one of the primary prerequisites both for a unified liberation campaign and for the establishment of an Indian nation. The fact that the leader of Bengal,

C.R. Das, was the first to achieve such a settlement, in 1924, a settlement which survived to the bitter end, won him Gandhiji's trust. Despite the most energetic of efforts Gandhiji did not succeed in reaching a similar settlement for the whole of India. It had been one of the first task that Gandhiji set for himself.

The first opportunity of any promise was presented after the First World War when the planned peace treaty between the Allies and Turkey made provisions for the dispersal of the Ottoman Empire, thus depriving the Sultan, in his capacity of Caliph, of the necessary foundations for his power. This then later led to his overthrow. Since they had no leader of their own faith, the Indian Muslims had become accustomed to seeing in the distant Caliph their own spiritual and worldly head and were extremely perturbed when they realised that his position was threatened by British Policy. A Muslim party was founded to save the Caliph, which was therefore anti-British in sentiment. Gandhiji at once seized this opportunity. Admittedly he was wise enough to realise that a campaign of this sort would be of no effect, since the Viceroy clearly did not conduct London's foreign policy, and he certainly did not overlook the fact that he was engaging his followers in a matter of indifference to the Hindus. Nevertheless he adopted the caliphate question as his own, declared the retention of the caliphate a commandment of the 'truth' and set his first great campaign this goal above all else. In this way he managed to unite both groups for the first time in an active front and to achieve for his own person a great measure of trust among the Muslims.

The political failure renewed the split between Muslims and Hindus; and all Gandhiji's attempts to bridge it remained fruitless, especially since Jinnah, the leader of the Muslim League who was now coming to power, was unable to show any understanding for Gandhiji and his ideas. The former's separatist tendencies, which aimed at severing a sovereign Muslim state from British Indian territory, became increasingly powerful, when he stayed as a guest at Jinnah's house and negotiated with him for over two weeks, did not alter his attitude.

Gandhiji, of course, was an opponent of the partition of India and spoke out against it to the last. He also saw more clearly than many others its consequences, the frightful riots in which the affected territories gave vent to their fear and hatred after news of the partition plan had been issued. It was here that Gandhiji found his last, hardest and most thankless task, a task that he heroically undertook at the age of 77. By frequently visiting their villages on foot, he tried to inspire with new courage those of both religions who were to suffer. In Bengal and Bihar he was more successful than an army of 50,000 men which was sent into restore order in the Punjab. Even in this situation his constant advice was for the Hindus to make concessions and to come to an honourable settlement with the Muslims. It was as a result of this that he was assassinated by a Hindu fanatic.

But it was precisely his death as a martyr which raised his reputation still further and really made him the 'Father of the Nation', Even in the early days and particularly in Africa, where he had encountered Indians of all backgrounds and shades of opinion, he had overcome his connections with his own people. On his return to India in 1915 he was one of the few politicians who felt themselves to be Indians, and Indians alone. But he also knew that a 'nation' cannot be constructed from an extremely divided population simply by means of speeches and gatherings. By appealing to all circles and groups of his people and extending the hand of brotherhood to every one of them without speaking of the nation or of nationalism, and by himself being a concrete example of how an Indian has to live, think and behave in modern times, he became the living symbol of the Indian nation, the universally revered father in whom everybody saw the head and the vital cohesive force of the new unity that was evolving. So it is that today his portrait hangs in the peasant's hut and the government office alike.

Gandhiji was alone and depressed on the great day of liberation, when the British flag was hauled down in Delhi. It was not a day of self-fulfilment for him. The separation of Pakistan and the bloody riots that followed in the border provinces which were to be surrendered, showed him that his life-long efforts to unify the whole people by means of education had been unsuccessful, in those parts at least. In the circle of his close friends he called the event a 'sorry affairs', for the way in which independence occurred was not as he had wished it. It was not the result of a *satyagraha* campaign which had involved the whole people, it had been forced on them from above, for in the final phase the British had been more eager to achieve withdrawal than the Indians, who argued more about the ways and the means. Indeed, in the end, at the request of the British, the transference of power was antedated a few months. The fact is that the majority of Indian leaders were taken by surprise, and in view of the inadequate state of preparation Gandhiji considered the date premature. He did not find his ideal realised in the new Indian state, for the broad mass of people were hardly liberated from oppression and misery at all.

As an old man, Gandhiji came to see that ideas, which he had largely formed in his early youth, did not form a suitable foundation for the nascent Indian state, the India of the future. He never possessed any clear conception of the 'state' and still less of the economy. The 'constitutional' road to freedom, which the majority of the politicians followed when reforms had given them the opportunity, was never accepted but grudgingly by Gandhiji. As his ideas were all based on the view that man is good and can be persuaded relatively simply to fulfil his duty, once he has gained the necessary insight, Gandhiji probably never understood that in practice many of these ideas could have led to anarchy, and that the state at least which the Indians now had to build up, needed to exercise more coercion and thus more 'violence' than he had imagined. Above all Gandhiji would most dearly have loved to transform India back into an agrarian state where the village would have formed the heart of public life. He thus failed to grasp the problem of how to deal with the rapidly growing population and inevitable dependence of India on foreign trade without appropriate new economic policies. During the struggle for freedom the spinning-wheel was an excellent method of providing everyone with an opportunity for helping in the task of liberation. It may even have been a blessing to remind many intellectuals of the value of their own skills in handicraft, but from now on its value was necessarily restricted to the narrow sphere of the village.

Even the service of the poor and the suffering, which Gandhiji had preached and exemplified, had to become a form of practical socialism now that the government was responsible for hundreds of millions. Machines, 'the work of the devil', were as necessary as trade unions and a planned economy, all things that Nehru had realised long before but which Gandhiji never really wanted to accept. What Gandhiji taught and strove for was at bottom a radical change in society that would put man above everything else. But what Gandhiji meant by man was an idealistic creation of whom there were but few examples in India. It was for this reason that much of what Gandhiji had rejected in his heart of hearts continued to exist both in the state structure and in the social order. To this extent he cannot be considered a revolutionary in Lenin's sense; on the contrary the British Indian Government frequently regarded him even as a bastion against radical trends. In the state that was now coming into being Gandhiji would have been a stranger and the tragedy that ended his life may in this sense have been a blessing for him.

As to what of him and of his spirit still live on in India today, it cannot be denied that he has moved into the background as regards the political practice of modern India. His followers regarded men like Jayaprakash Narayan or Vinoba Bhave as genuine 'Gandhians'. Jayaprakash Narayan was perhaps the most gifted politician of the Nehru generation and, thanks to his great personal ability, he managed to become both the loyal disciple of Gandhiji and a close friend of Nehru. The latter had originally selected Jayaprakash Narayan as his successor, until he withdrew from the political scene, an embittered man. Outside India the best 'Gandhian' was considered to be Martin Luther King, the leader of the American negroes who shared both Gandhiji's non-violent methods and his tragic end.

What will history show to have been his role ? It cannot be disputed that it was he who provided the Indian Liberation Movement with the energy and the broad base that patently made an impression on India's British rulers. Without Gandhiji this movement would never have reached the intensity that it did. He mobilised the Indian masses, and it was the example of the success that they achieved which in turn aroused all the other coloured colonial peoples of Asia and Africa. Indeed it was Gandhiji himself who sowed the first seeds in South Africa. Gandhiji had no racial complexes but he can hardly have forgotten the night that he spent alone freezing on a South African railway station after he had been forcibly ejected from his compartment and then expected to travel on in the luggage van, despite the fact that he had a valid first-class ticket. He resolved to fight against any such racial injustices on behalf of a true equality of all races. This revolt against injustice and violence was a more powerful motive force within him even than his resistance against British colonial rule, for he always remained free of any hostility or hatred in his personal relationships with Britain and the British. Not even, the years spent in British prisons altered this attitude, a characteristic that also applied to Nehru. It was precisely the non-violence which he employed, as opposed to the assassinations carried out by the Indian underground movement, which made it possible for British rule to come to a close without any bloodshed being split between the Indians and their former masters.

Equally undisputable is Gandhiji's decisive share in the unification of the population of the Indian subcontinent, in short his share in the birth of an Indian nation. Certainly he never said much about the nation or about nationalism but he provided the people with that inner experience which produced the feeling that they all shared common destiny. This was one of the most lasting effects of his work and especially of his last campaign, the 'Quit India' movement. However, much one may wonder just how politically opportune this movement was, the riots and disturbances that ensued, and above all, the mass street demonstrations by the women of India, gave everyone a profound sense of common purpose.

In the analysis history will praise Gandhiji for two major achievements: in the first place this man who came to lead a great nation was a politician of quite exceptional honesty and selflessness—something which also speaks for the country that recognised him. This was a man of iron self-discipline who expected an equally high moral standard of his followers, and these two qualities were vital both in attracting to the cause circles that were by no means in complete agreement with him, and in inspiring the masses, to whom political activity was still entirely alien, with the spirit of sacrifice and the courage that could alone inject his movement with necessary strength to make a decisive impression on the British colonial rulers.

In the second place history will recognise that despite the rigidity with which he adhered to his own ideas he sensed or foresaw that after him other methods and different kinds of political leaders would be required. One of his most fruitful and wisest political decisions will always be seen as his choice of younger man from the next generation as his successor, a man who did not agree with him in certain essential points and who, in spite of personal loyalty to him as a fatherly friend and leader, was determined to adopt many different policies once their goal had been attained. Thus Gandhiji closed that era of India that will bear his name in reconciliatory and intelligent manner, and gave new India his blessing in advance.

Gandhiji played a crucial role in the struggle for Indian freedom, providing leadership to it for nearly thirty years. His significance in history rests not on his role as a conciliator, but on his commitment to struggle, not merely for national freedom but also for the establishment of a just social order. To him, violence is always preferable to cowardice. The masses as well as a majority of the political workers and leaders at various levels were drawn towards him. To quote B.R. Nanda, "Gandhiji was now the Mahatma, the great soul; with his voluntary poverty, simplicity, humility and saintliness he seemed a *Rishi* (sage) of old who had stepped from the pages of an ancient epic to bring about the liberation of his country".

The government's report on the political situation in India in 1919 noted: the combination of these three factors, the uneasiness of the politically-minded, the anxiety of the advanced Muhammadans, the distress of the masses, was to create a situation fraught with the most dangerous possibilities of internal order. In short, there was to be noticed on the part of the politicians, a determination to assert themselves, to enforce their claims, and to impress Government with the impossibility of ignoring their position and influence. And it was the existence of specific and particular grievances, such as the pro-Turkish sentiment among advanced Muhammadans and economic suffering among the lower classes, which tended to transmute this feeling of disquiet into a definitely anti-Government attitude.

No established political party or leader came forward to show the way during Rowlatt bills. In these circumstances Gandhiji came forward with his call for *satyagraha* in the event of the Rawlatt bills becoming law. The spectacular, though uneven, response to this call in various parts of the country marked the emergence of Gandhiji as the dominant figure in Indian politics. To quote Jawaharlal Nehru,

> "The Amritsar Congress was the first Gandhi Congress. Lokmanya Tilak was also present and took a prominent part in the deliberations, but there could be no doubt about it that the majority of the delegates, and even more so the great crowds outside, looked to Gandhi for leadership. The slogan Mahatma Gandhi Ki Jai began to dominate the Indian political horizon".

Gandhiji acquired this position in 1919 because he fulfilled a major need of the political situation in India. He caught the attention of the majority of the politically conscious sections of the Indian people in 1919 because he showed the path to peaceful but effective action. It was not his non-violence which was new, but the message of fearlessness and the call for non-violent action or struggle. Nehru explained the emergence of Gandhiji: First World War ended at last, and the peace, instead of bringing us relief and progress, brought us repressive legislation and martial law in the Punjab. A bitter sense of humiliation and a passionate anger filled our people. We seemed to be helpless in the grip of some all powerful monster; our limbs were paralysed, our minds deadened. And then Gandhi came. He was like a powerful current of fresh air that made us stretch ourselves and take deep breaths; like a beam of light that pierced the darkness and removed the scales from our eyes; like a whirlwind that upset many things, but most of all working of people's minds. He did not descend from the top; he seemed to emerge from the millions of India, speaking their language, and incessantly drawing attention to them and their appalling condition. The essence of his teaching was fearlessness and truth, and action allied to these, always keeping the welfare of the masses in view.

The crisis of leadership which the Congress and the country was facing in 1919 and which enabled Gandhiji to ascend to the top had not arisen all of a sudden. The outbreak of the first world war accentuated the crisis of leadership in the Indian nationalist movement. The passing away of Gokhale in 1915, created a major void in Indian public life. To quote Aurobindo Ghosh.

> "All great movements wait for their God-sent leader, the willing channel of force, and only when he comes, move forward triumphantly to their fulfilment. The men who have led hitherto have been strong men of high gifts and commanding genius, great enough to be the protagonists of any other movement, but even they were not sufficient to fulfil one which is the chief current of a world-wide revolution. Therefore, the nationalist party, custodians of the future, must wait for the man who is to come, calm in the midst of calamity, hopeful under defeat, sure of eventual emergence and triumph and always mindful of the responsibility which they owe not only to their Indian posterity but to the world".

Gandhiji published *Hind Swaraj* in 1909. The publication of *Hind Swaraj* clearly shows that 'as early as 1909 Gandhiji was ready for the moment when the finger of destiny would beckon him to assume the leadership of the Indian national movement'. By 1909 he was well-known enough for his name to be proposed by the Bengal Provincial Congress Committee for the Presidentship of the annual Congress session to be held at the end of the year.

Gokhale paid glowing tributes to Gandhiji. He said, "The Indian cause in South Africa has really been built up by Mr. Gandhi. Without self, and without strain, he has fought his great fight for this country during a period now of twenty years and India owes an immense debt of gratitude to him. He was sacrificed himself entirely to the service of the cause". Gokhale's visit to South Africa symbolised the deep interest of the Indian people in the struggle of their brethren in that land under Gandhi's leadership. By the time Gandhiji returned to India in 1915 there was already in existence here a powerful Gandhi legend. Gandhiji remained only on the periphery of the political circle in India and continued to be known primarily as a hero of the Indian struggle in South Africa, without much interest in Indian politics. To quote Nehru, "All of us admired him for his heroic fight in South Africa, but he seemed very distant and different and unpolitical to many of us young men. He refused to take part in Congress or national politics then and confined himself to the South African Indian questions".

An invitation from the peasants in the district of Champaran in Bihar, provided the first major opportunity to Gandhiji to test his technique of struggle (*satyagraha*) and project its efficacy before the general public. The long struggle in South Africa as well as the local struggles in India which Gandhiji had till then led had already powerfully projected his image of a fighter among the elite as well as the masses. It was the combination of that image with Gandhiji's courage in challenging the might of the imperial government, almost single-handed, without the support of any major organisation or party, and with the explosive political situation in India after the end of the First Word War which produced the spectacular response all over the country and marked emergence of Gandhiji as the dominant figure in Indian politics.

Gandhiji evolved his basic strategy on the basis partly of his understanding of the nature of British rule in India and partly of his study of popular movements both in India and abroad during the first decade of the twentieth century. He realised that in order to free India from British rule what was necessary was to free the Indian people from the awe of British institutions and to instill in them a pride of their own civilisation and culture. Whatever might have been said by Gandhiji regarding the conversion of the government, the main objective of *satyagraha* was to bring about a change in the attitude of the people at large. It is their conversion that really mattered. Whenever there was a gesture of conciliation from the government he thought that as a *satyagrahi* it was his duty to respond with a similar gesture provided it was possible to do so without giving up any of the essentials of his position. It was in keeping with this principle that he negotiated the Gandhi-Irwin Agreement in 1931 and made so many attempts on various occasions for a settlement with Britain.

One of the keys to the continuance as well as emergence of Gandhi's leadership was his supreme sense of tactics. He knew when to start a movement and when to suspend it. Till 1942 his decisions were always accepted, though not on occasions without much argument and questioning, by a majority of the various organs of the Congress. Gandhiji said, "A leader is useless when he acts against the prompting of his own conscience, surrounded as he must be by people holding all kinds of views. He will drift like an anchorless ship, if he has not the inner voice to hold him firm and guide him". In 1939, he said, "In a *satyagraha* campaign the mode of fight and the choice of tactics, e.g., whether to advance or retreat, offer civil resistance or organise non-violent strength through constructive work and purely selfless humanitarian service are determined according to the exigencies of the situation". It was his estimate of the 'exigencies of a situation' which guided him in all his decisions regarding when to start and when to suspend civil disobedience. He himself took all the major decisions regarding suspending a struggle often to the dismay of his colleagues.

After his arrival in India in 1915 and while working his way to national leadership, Gandhiji took up the cause of peasants and industrial workers. He did not give up his interest in peasants and workers after reaching that destination. On the contrary, he always emphasised the supreme importance of Congress leaders and workers identifying themselves with the poor and working for their uplift.

Gandhiji and Nehru worked together in gradually changing the economic policy and outlook of the Congress. Gandhiji was all the time preparing the ground for committing the Congress to the establishment of an egalitarian order by emphasising that it must give the greatest attention to the interests of the poor. The new ideology which gradually developed between 1936 and 1947 had a marked socialist orientation. The shift from capitalism to socialism was clearly there, although that shift had not been fully completed by the time independence came and the Congress had to face a new situation. The shift from capitalism to socialism in the Congress ideology during the last decade before the achievement of independence was, of course, not directly led by Gandhiji, but by Nehru and the leaders of the Congress Socialist Party founded in 1934.

Gandhiji always extended his patronage and backing to Nehru and the Congress Socialist leaders, particularly their chief spokesman,

Jayaprakash Narayan and shielded them from the attacks of his constructive followers. Thus Gandhiji had been mainly instrumental in getting Nehru, whose socialist inclinations were already well-known, elected as president of the Congress in 1929. In January 1942 Gandhiji openly declared in course of speech before the All India Committee that he had been saying for years that Nehru would be his successor. Gandhiji adopted a similar attitude towards the leaders of the Congress Socialist Party. When Jayaprakash Narayan was arrested in March 1940 for one of his speeches opposing the use of Indian resources for the British war effort, Gandhiji described the government's action as 'unfortunate'.

Gandhiji openly described himself as an old socialist and affirmed his acceptance of socialist principles provided they were sought to be implemented through non-violence. He said, "I have claimed that I was a socialist long before those I know in India had avowed their creed. But my socialism was natural to me and not adopted from any books. It came out of my unshakable belief in non-violence. No man could be actively non-violent and not rise against social injustice no matter where it occurred". Indeed as time passed he felt himself closer and closer to both socialism and the Congress socialist leaders. As he repeatedly declared, his difference with the socialists related only to the use of violence in bringing about socialism. In 1940, he said, "In spite of the utmost effort, the rich do not become guardians of the poor in the true sense of the term and the latter are more and more crushed and die of hunger what is to be done? In trying to find out the solution to this riddle I have lighted on non-violent non-cooperation and civil disobedience as the right and infallible means. The rich cannot accumulate wealth without the cooperation of the poor in society. If this knowledge were to penetrate and spread amongst the poor, they would become strong and would learn how to free themselves by means of non-violence from the crushing inequalities which have brought them to the verge of starvation".

Gandhiji was not merely tried to endow the Indian nationalist movement with an egalitarian social outlook, but also placed before it the vision of a new world free from international conflicts based on mutual cooperation among nations. Indeed the dominant conscious urge of Indian nationalism under Gandhiji's leadership was not isolation but international cooperation. India's decision to remain in the Commonwealth after the achievement of independence was largely the result of Gandhian approach to international relations. Gandhiji anticipated several other major components of India's foreign policy. Thus he looked forward to Asian resurgence and unity in 1920. He did not show any interest in establishing India's hegemony over her small neighbours in Asia. On the contrary, he showed interest in promoting their independent nationhood. Gandhiji never ceased emphasising that as India was carrying on her freedom through non-violent means she would be specially suited to work for the maintenance of peace in the world, which was her true mission. In the forties he became growingly concerned with the growth of violence and piling of armaments in different parts of the world and became more and more convinced that the only way to save the world from total destruction was to adopt the path of non-violence.

Gandhiji's leadership became indispensable and in September 1940, the All-India Congress Committee adopted a resolution, obviously drafted by Nehru, clarifying its stand on the issue of non-violence. Gandhiji was obviously not happy with the working committee's refusal to commit itself to non-violence in foreign and defence policies, but saw its difficulty and actually commended its resolution before the All-India Congress Committee which met soon after, in January, 1942. At the same time Gandhiji also made his own position clear and declared that he would not like to exchange non-violence even for independence and would not like to participate in war, but to work for peace. Though Gandhiji continued to lay stress on India's mission to work for peace in the world he never again insisted on the Congress sticking to non-violence in defence or foreign policy if it was to retain his leadership.

One of the distinctive marks of Gandhiji's leadership was his extraordinary organisational ability. In South Africa he built up a powerful organisation of Indian settlers from the scratch. In India, once he emerged as the undisputed leader of the Congress he revolutionised its structure and functioning. The Congress under him became a much more powerful organisation than it had ever been before or could be after his passing away. Gandhiji made the Congress as a mass organisation. He always remained watchful and alert and keen to encourage the right kind of talent whenever he spotted it, both by assigning responsibility and by placing it in limelight. He maintained a close personal relationship with a large number of followers and tried to inspire them to do their best for the country. The supreme power in the Congress organisation as well as in the movements which he had always remained with him till 1942.

August 1942 showed Gandhiji at his best as the leader of the Indian struggle for freedom. 1942 saw not only Gandhiji's finest hour, but also his last. When the movement he had led since 1919-20 reached its final phase in 1946-47, his leadership suffered a clear decline and almost collapsed. He, of course, continued to be defined by the masses as never before. Crowds wishing to have his *darshan* continued to swell. Shouts of *Mahatma Gandhiji Ki Jai* continued to rent the air. But Gandhiji was no longer the chief factor in decision-making inside the Congress, which he had dominated since 1919-20, and which was now engaged in taking momentous decision regarding the future of the country.

Gandhiji was not at all sympathetic and wanted the British Government to quit the country leaving the issue of partition to be decided by Indian themselves without the presence of the British power. The voice of Gandhiji, however, became more and more a voice in the wilderness. The Congress leaders, entrenched in seats of power and looking forward to the achievement of independence through a negotiated settlement, no longer treated Gandhiji's leadership as indispensable and were even prepared to take their own decisions without consulting Gandhiji. It is obvious that the Congress leaders no longer considered it necessary to consult Gandhiji before taking an important decision and were also not interested in explaining it to him afterwards.

Gandhiji was present at the meeting of the Working Committee, but the decision to accept partition was taken against his wishes. While Gandhiji spent his time addressing prayer meetings and applying the healing touch to the victims of communal riots in Bihar, his chief lieutenants, Nehru and Patel, were busy in settling the terms of the partition and getting the first draft of the Mountbatten Plan, as amended by the British Cabinet, suitably revised to safeguard the interests of what was to be left as India after partition. Gandhiji was not consulted about such matters and had no idea of the shaping of the Mountbatten Plan in which Nehru had played a key role, but had shared his secret initially only with Patel and at a later stage with few other leaders like Rajendra Prasad, Maulana Azad and Kripalani.

What irked Gandhiji was the way partition was being brought about. His deep agony at the thought of partition under British supervision, in the midst of widespread Hindu-Muslim rioting, came out through words uttered before his personal entourage that evening: "My life's work seems to be over. I hope God will spare me further humiliation".

There is no doubt that the failure to prevent partition did not mean the end of Gandhiji's leadership, but it was a leadership shorn of the power he had wielded between 1920 and 1946 and now functioned merely through moral influence. Thus there is a basic difference between the Gandhiji of 1920-46 and that of 1946-48. Gandhiji stood like a rock in the vast sea of communal hatred and ill-will surrounding on all sides, and continued to preach, as heroically as ever before, the message of communal harmony and goodwill. While Gandhiji's role as a preacher of communal harmony and goodwill is important, his place in history really rests on his unique leadership of the Indian struggle for freedom. The record of Gandhiji as a political leader is not one of success only, but also includes a major failure—the failure to keep India united.

Gandhiji was, beyond any doubt, the greatest in the galaxy of leaders produced by the Indian nationalist movement. At the world stage he takes his place by the side of Lenin as one of the two leaders whose achievements have had the greatest impact on the history of our times. If Lenin spearheaded the workers' revolution, Gandhiji spearheaded the anti-colonial revolution. The character of his leadership played a major role in strengthening the roots of democracy in India.

Gandhiji was the leader of a national liberation movement and developed the technique of *satyagraha*, based on truth and non-violence, for challenging the mightiest empire in history. He wanted society to be reconstructed on the basis of the principles of justice, equality and freedom. He had the task of mobilising a whole nation for securing its deliverance from foreign rule. It was necessary for him to strengthen the pride of the Indian people in their own cultural heritage. He became a symbol of India's pride as well as of her determination to be free. He was not only a charismatic leader and supreme political strategist, but also a great organiser. Under his guidance the Congress acquired a far-flung organisation touching all parts of the country and encompassing in it almost all sections of the Indian people. His flair for spotting talented persons and providing them with suitable training as well as opportunities for leadership was an important aspect of his organisational capacity.

Gandhiji attached great importance to the liberty of the individual, the enjoyment by him of the freedom of speech, expression and association, the complete absence of any discrimination between citizens on the basis of caste, religion or sex, the rule of law and the supremacy of the civil over the military authority. He looked forward to the ultimate emergence of a system of democracy which would be free from the clash of political parties and in which all citizens would cooperate among themselves, keeping only the good of the society in mind. He realised that this was basically an utopian ideal, not likely to be practised in practice, at any rate in the foreseeable future. He attached importance to the proper growth of political parties, did not favour any party's monopoly of the political field and wanted the fullest possible freedom to be given to all the political parties to propagate their views.

Gandhiji stood for the establishment of a system which would free society from the curse of poverty and exploitation and provide equal opportunities to all its members. He wanted the means of production, distribution and exchange to be under social control and the profit motive and the acquisitive tendency among the individuals to be kept under check. His theory of trusteeship was not a shield for the protection of vested interests, but a device to sweeten the bitter pill of social control over all the common wealth produced in society.

4

ON RELIGION

Gandhiji's political philosophy cannot be discussed except in relation to his concepts of truth, duty and non-violence, and his vision about man, society and state. At the apex of his beliefs is the Hindu concept *of Satya*. Allied to *satya* in Gandhiji's system of beliefs is his conception of law or duty which in Hindu thought is conveyed by the word *dharma*. He generally tended to understand *dharma* as universal morality to which the affairs of men and state should correspond. However, his basic ideas included not only satya and *dharma* but also *ahimsa* as understood by Vaishnavism, Jainism and Buddhism. He was convinced that man's first duty stems from his relation to the higher law of *dharma*. But he also believed that no political, social or religious institution is needed to interpret *dharma*. Man best performs his duty by working from subjective, personal reform to objective interpersonal and institutional reform in society, the state and the world. To his mind social and political theories and reforms must receive light and guidance from moral principles which, however, are the expressions of the ultimate truth in tangible form.

Gandhiji's religion is the religion of truth. That is why he respected all the religions alike. The religious conflict according to him is only a passing phenomena, and not a permanent one. The religious conflicts are due to mutual distrust among the followers of various religions and fear of other religions. He was not at all interested in the superficial ceremonies and traditions. His interest was the essence of religion, that is, truth and non-violence. When people fought in the name of religion, he was shocked and painfully expressed that the real purpose of religion is to unite man with truth and love. Real religious understanding makes people to live with each other like brothers. He repeatedly said that unity of religions is not on the basis of mutual fear but on the basis of mutual love and understanding.

Gandhiji proclaimed himself as a Sanatani Hindu. But he was not a dogmatic follower of Hinduism. In his earlier days, when he heard the irregularity of the temple priests, he disliked visits to temples. When he was asked to take bath, after touching his play-mate, who was supposed to be untouchable, he reacted. When religious men opposed his foreign travel on the basis of scriptures, he followed the reason and disobeyed them. These incidents indicate the development of religion in him which is the love of reason and not dogmatism.

Gandhiji's understanding of Hinduism never compelled him to oppose any other religion but helped him to learn the good aspects of all the major religions of the world. He not only believed in the fundamental spiritual tenets of Hinduism, but he accepted all religions to be equally true. He accepted the moral and spiritual essence of Hinduism, which according to him, was the essence of all the religions of the mankind. In short, he believed in genuine religious fellowship and fraternity and his synthetic mind observed points of common fundamental ethical significance in all the scriptures of the world. It is the concept of religion as dynamic altruism that he wanted to make the basis for the transformation of social and political actions.

Gandhiji's religion is a religion of morality and spirituality. It is not the religion of ritualism and dogmatism. That is why he moved with different religious people and studied deeply different religious books. His problem was not to bring all the religions into Hinduism, but living in a harmonious way without changing his own faith. He emphasised tolerance as the basic qualities of a religious man because truth is one and God is one. All the religions have glimpses of truth within them. So one must give respect to other faiths in order to spiritual insight from the different religions.

Man's goal is not only to lead a religious life but to know the eternal truth which is beyond all the religions. The different religions are different means. One must not fight in the name of religion. One must live a honest, a truthful life to know the truth. Gandhiji said that he learnt the different aspects of religions not from their features but from the surroundings. The term religion to him is different from the usual meaning. In his younger days he moved with the people of various religions. When he listened to the priest of Christianity addressing the people as sinners, he hated the religion of priest. When people of Christianity changed the traditional dresses and ate beef and drank liquor he hated their practices. Later on, when he went to England, he changed all his misunderstanding about Christianity. He understood the real spirit of Christianity when he read the *Sermon on the Mount.*

Gandhiji accepted the creative and stupendous force of religion in human history and was primarily concerned with the ethical aspects of religion and spoke of religion in terms of ethical idealism. He said, "For me morals, ethics and religion are convertible terms. A moral life without reference to religion is like a house built upon sand. And religion divorced from morality is like sounding brass, food only for making noise and breaking heads". All religions are founded on the same moral laws.

Gandhiji studied different religions of the world in a spirit of open mindedness and found that the moral element was common to all religions, signifying the unity of all religions. That the ethics of piety, forgiveness, humanity, tolerance, compassion and love should influence political activities is the basic view of Gandhiji. He himself practised the moral virtues and wanted that they should be practised by all in social and political fields.

Gandhiji always spoke of religion in terms of ethical idealism and regarded spiritual perfection as only the consummation of moral endeavours. Religion signified, to him, belief in the ordered moral governance of the world and the spirit of faith dependence upon the absolute truth. Hence it demanded a complete consecration of a man's being and personality to truth which is God and implied an emphasis on the moral values of man. He always talked of ethical religion. As soon as the moral basis is lost one ceases to be religious. *Karmayoga* rooted in *Anasakti* is the essence of his ethical religion. The true religious attitude means the voluntary acceptance and the enthusiastic fulfilment of the duties that naturally come one's way. In his writings there is emphasis on the pursuit of universalist percepts and maxims in place of caste duties and obligations. He thus seeks substitute scriptural positivism by moral universalism. In the spirit of the *Gita*, he felt that persued with a sense of detachment and equanimity the life of *Karmayoga* could lead to the attainment of *Moksha.*

Gandhiji was one of the personalities of India who believed that religion is a creative force in life. He was very much to develop the ethical basis of religion. To him, religion must necessarily be pragmatic. A multi-religious society struggling for socio-political progress needs an all embracing conception of religion which can bind people of divergent faiths together for a joint march towards a new social reconstruction. He does not believe that religious affairs can be kept divorced from political affairs. He said that religion which takes no account of practical affairs and does not help to solve them, is no religion. Religion, for him is a living faith which derives sustenance from devotion to a spiritual being which is most fully revealed to us as truth. He believes that religion is always subject to a process of evolution and re-interpretation. Progress towards truth, towards God, is possible only because of such evolution.

Gandhiji was primarily a social reformer who preached everything for the benefit of the human society. To him, religion has got practical importance in life. He tried to spiritualise all aspects of human life. His concept of religion is wide, tolerant and comprehensive. The application of the scientific methods to the field of religion strikes at the very root of the meaning and significance of religion. Religion is the basic need of a man. It is instinctive and impulsive. It has rooted in our nature and is as old as weeping or smiling. But the term 'religion' has, however, been variedly conceived and is therefore, liable to be misconceived too. Religion entails many things and even if one single element of it is taken to mean the whole of it, we are sure to miss the truth. Religion means a belief in a personal God in whom our being or existence is rooted. It can be defined as knowledge of God and an emotional practical relationship with Him. The purpose of human existence and the goal of life can be sought through religion alone. It is religion which alone can assure us of everlasting joy and peace. It is primarily concerned with the redemption of evils.

In the ordinary sense of the term, religion is man's cognitive, affective, and conative attitude to his environment and to the universe as a whole, chiefly determined by his instinctive and intuitive faith, which gets stabilised in tradition. In spite of the progress in the science, still man lacks an integration within himself and in adjustment to and in harmony with his national and social environment. He needs a new vision, a new feeling and a new motive, which may save him and make him happy. This is expected to come from religion.

Religion is the spiritual need of a man. It is an attempt on the part of the human-being to comprehend that reality which lied beyond the orbits of the world of observation. It is an endeavour on the part of the finite to know, understand and realise the Infinite. It is a unique effort of the finite to experience the Infinites. It is a way which the finite treads to be in tune with the Infinite. It is the very core of religion. There cannot be any religion without the element of spirituality. The purpose of religion is to know the unknown in the realm of known, to see the unseen in the world of the seen and to realise the self in the religion of the non-self. It is a path as well as the method of acquiring the knowledge of the Invisible beyond the visible; the knowledge of the Infinite beyond the finite and the Knowledge of the imperceptible beyond the perceptible.

According to Dr. S. Radhakrishnan, "Comparative religion proves beyond doubt that while there are innumerable changes in religious forms, religion itself is found to be a universal phenomena. Right around the world, distributed more or less uniformly, we find a mass of faith and ritual which, inspite of apparent variations and individual forms, seem to cohere with respect to certain essential features. Religion is native to the human mind, integral to human nature itself. Everything else may dissolve; but belief in God, which is the ultimate confession of all the faiths of the world, remains. Though remains may take many forms, it will continue, as long as man remains what he is, a blend of power and weakness".

To quote R.C. Zaehner, "The endowment of a chair in Eastern Religions and Ethics was an act of faith. It was an expression not only of Mr. and Mrs. Spalding's faith, in an ultimate unity underlying all the great religions but to their faith in the University of Oxford as a suitable channel through which to make these outlandish systems more widely known. It was, however, more than an act of faith; it was an act of statesmanship. For it showed a keen realisation on the part of Mr. and Mrs. Spalding that any view of world history which was based exclusively on the European contribution must be, to some extent, lop-sided. For they realised, earlier than most of us, that Asia, so long the unwilling ward of Europe, could not for ever be subjected to an alien way of life and an alien way of thought. They understand that it is not possible for one culture permanently to be imposed on another, and that sooner or later the cultures of Europe and Asia would have to meet on equal terms".

According to Max Muller, "I hold that there is a divine element in every one of the great religions of the world. I consider it blasphemous to call them the work of the devil, when they are the work of God; and I hold that there is nowhere any belief in God except spirit working in man. I could not call myself a Christian if I were to believe otherwise, if I were to force myself against all my deepest instincts, to believe that the prayers of Christians were the only prayers that God could understand. All religions are mere stammerings, our own as much as that of the Brahmins. They all have to be translated; and I have no doubt they all will be translated whatever their shortcomings may be".

Universal religion is the fruit of the merger of religions. And all religions must meet in the same spirit if they really want to achieve something. Dr. S. Radhakrishnan said, "The different religions have now come together and if they are not to continue in a state of conflict or competition, they must develop a spirit of comprehension which will break down prejudice and misunderstanding and bind them together as varied expressions of a single truth. Such a spirit characterised the development of Hinduism, which has not been interrupted for nearly fifty centuries. The past strength and continuity of Hindu culture, as well as its present weakness and disorder, are problems of equal interest. Nor does the weakness really contradict the strength. Hinduism is not based on any racial factor. It is an inheritance of thought and, aspiration to which every race in India has based its distinctive contribution."

Gandhiji believed that religion is a creative force in life. He was very much to develop the ethical basis of religion. The multiplicity of religions created some peculiar problems to the Indian people and they turned to secularism in order to find a solution for those problems. To him, religion must necessarily be pragmatic. He did not accept traditional or conventional religion.. He did not adhere to any religious principle uncritically. He was influenced by the Eastern and Western religious thinkers. He dedicated his life to the service of the masses, which was the essence of his religion. Religion is the basis on which all life structure has to be erected, if life is to be complete. No man can live without religion.

Gandhiji used the term 'religion' in a wider sense. He held that religion is a term of wide connotations. He inherited his religious forum from his parents. His family background shaped his religious thought to a certain extent. He said, "Of religious training he had very little, but he had that kind of religious culture by frequent visits to temples and listening to religious discourses made available to many Hindus. In his last days, he began reading the *Gita* at the instance of a learned Brahmin friend of the family, and he used to repeat aloud some verses everyday at the time of worship".

Gandhiji was also influenced by his mother, Putlibai. He said, "The outstanding impression that my mother has left on my memory is that of saintliness. She would not think of taking her meals without her daily prayers. Going to Haveli—the Vaishnava temple—was one of her daily duties".

The epic *Ramayana* left an impression on Gandhiji's spiritual thought. He said, "What however, left a deep impression on me was the reading of the *Ramayana* before my father. During part of his illness, my father was in Porbandar. There every evening he used to listen to the *Ramayana*. The reader was a great devotee of Rama. I must have been thirteen at that time, but I quite remember being enraptured by his reading. That laid the foundation of my deep devotion to the *Ramayana*".

The family atmosphere of Gandhiji was also responsible for his religious fervour. He said, "In Rajkot, however I got an early grounding in toleration for all branches of Hinduism and sister religions. For my father and mother would visit the Haveli as also Shiva's and Rama's temples, and would take or send us (youngsters) there. Jain monks also would pay frequent visits to my father. They would have talks with my father on subjects—religious and mundane. Besides he had Mosalman and Parsi friends, who would talk to him about their own faiths, and he would listen to them always with respect, and often with interest. Being his nurse, I often had a chance to be present at those talks. These many things combined to inculcate in me a toleration for all faiths".

According to P.F. Power, "Other religious philosophies touched him during his childhood, but especially Jainism. This is a reform group external to orthodox Hinduism and composed mainly of urban trading classes. Jains search for ultimate truth beyond the senses and take a vow of non-injury to avoid harm to all living things, including micro-organisms. This pledge of personal non-violence is *ahimsa*, found also in Buddhism and Hinduism as a virtue of the man who renounces the world. Under different influences Gandhiji later reinterpreted and expanded this principle to include temporal and collective as well as spiritual and individual matters". To quote Louis Fischer, "Gandhi was always a great observer. Jainism, as well as Buddhism, perceptibly coloured Gandhiji's thoughts and shaped his works".

Gandhiji's religious thought was also moulded by *Manusmriti*. He said, "But the fact that I had learnt to be tolerant to other religions did not mean that I had any living faith in God. I happened about this time to come across *Manusmriti* which was amongst my father's collection. The story of the creation and similar things did not impress me very much, but on the contrary made me incline somewhat towards atheism. But one thing took deep root in me—the conviction that morality is the basis of things, and that truth is the substance of all morality. Truth became my sole objective.

It began to grow in magnitude every day, my definition of it also has been ever widening".

Gandhiji was very much influenced by Jainism. The Jains traditions and the contact with Raychandbhai helped him very much. He said, "I have tried to meet the heads of various faiths, and I must say that no one else has ever made on me the impression that Raychandbhai did. His words went straight home to me. His intellect compelled as great a regard from me as his moral earnestness. In my moments of spiritual crisis, therefore, he was my refuge".

Buddhism also influenced Gandhiji's religious thought. He said, "The brothers also recommended the *Light of Asia* by Sir Edwin Arnold, whom I know till then as the author only of *The Song Celestial*, and I read it with even greater interest than I did the *Bhagvadgita*. Once I had begun it I could not leave off".

Gita also influenced Gandhiji. He said, "The impression has ever since been growing on me with the result that I regard it today as the book par excellence for the knowledge of Truth. Renunciation in action is the message of the *Gita*. It is a book of spiritual reference to me. . . . But after forty years unremitting endeavour fully to enforce the teaching of the *Gita* in my own life, I have in all humility, felt that perfect renunciation is impossible without perfect observance of *ahimsa* in every shape and form". The *Gita* inspires us to do our duties, neglecting the suffering and the torture that we receive in course of our action. He said, "This is the unmistakable teaching of the *Gita*. He who gives up action falls. He who gives up only the reward rises. But renunciation of fruit in no way means indifference to the result. In regard to every action, one must know the result that is expected to follow, the means thereto, and the capacity for it. He, who, being thus equipped, is without desire for the result and is yet wholly engrossed in the due fulfilment of the task before him is said to have renounced the fruits of his action".

According to Louis Fischer, "There are devout Hindus, and mystic Hindus, who sit and meditate and fast and go naked and live in the Himalayan cave. But Gandhi aimed to be ever active, ever useful and even needless. This was the realisation he craved. Like everybody else Gandhi had attachment. He sought to slough them off". To quote Gandhiji, "He (the author of the *Gita*) has drawn no line of demarcation between salvation and worldly pursuits. On the contrary, he has shown that religion must rule even our worldly pursuits. I have felt that the *Gita* teaches us that cannot be followed out in day-to-day practice cannot be called religion".

Christianity also influenced Gandhiji's religious thought. The 'Sermon on the Mount' especially created an indelible impression on his mind. He said, "I have not been able to see any difference between the *Sermon on the Mount* and the *Bhagvadgita*. What the Sermon describes in graphic manner, the *Bhagvadgita* reduces to a scientific formula. It may not be a scientific book in the accepted sense of term, but it has argued out the law of love—the law of abandon as I call it—in a scientific manner. The *Sermon on the Mount* gives the same law in the wonderful language. Today, supposing, I was deprived of the *Gita* and forgot all its contents but had a copy of the Sermons, I should derive the same joy from it as I do from the *Gita*".

The major religions of the world influenced Gandhiji and shaped his course of life. He said, "My young mind tried to unify the teaching of the *Gita*, the *Light of Asia* and the *Sermon on the Mount*. That renunciation was the highest form of religion appealed to me greatly".

Regarding religion, Gandhiji said, "Let me explain what I mean by religion. It is not the Hindu religion which I certainly prize above all other religions, but the religion which transcends Hinduism, which changes one's very nature, which binds one indissolubly to the truth within and which ever purifies. It is the permanent element in human nature which counts no cost too great in order to find full expression and which leaves the soul utterly restless until it has found itself, known its Maker and appreciated the true correspondence between the Maker and itself". By religion, he does not mean formal religion, or customary religion, but that religion which underlies all religions, which brings us face to face with our Maker. Religion should pervade every one of our actions. Here religion does not mean sectarianism. It means a belief in ordered moral government of the universe. It is not less real because it is unseen. This religion transcends Hinduism, Islam, Christianity, etc. It does not supersede them. It harmonises them and gives them reality.

According to Gandhiji, "No man can live without religion. There are some, who, in the egotism of their reason declare that they have nothing to do with religion. But it is like a man saying that he breathes but that he has no nose whether by reason, or by instinct, or by superstition, man acknowledges some sort of relationship with the divine. The rankest agnostic or atheist does acknowledge the need of a moral principle, and associates something good with its observance and something but with its non-observance.

Bradleaugh, whose atheism is well known, always insisted on proclaiming his innermost conviction. He had to suffer a lot for thus speaking the truth, but he delighted in it and said that truth is its own reward. Not that he was quite insensible to the joy resulting from the observance of truth. This joy however is not all worldly, but springs out of communion with the divine. That is why I have said that even a man who disowns religion cannot and does not live without religion".

The following principles may be considered as the essence of all religions:

1. There is faculty of power in man deeper than his senses and intellect. A high quotient of this faculty makes one a religious prophet.
2. Underlying and pervading all the multiple forms of beings, there is a Unitary being, which is richer than all its manifestations, emanations or creations, which is the source, the support and the goal of all beings.
3. We are more than sensations and intellect can think of.
4. Every man is responsible for his own good or bad actions, the consequences of which he has to bear.
5. The moment one consciously tries to surrender and sacrifice his self interest for the service and good of his fellow beings in devotion to God, his heart begins to the inflow of Divine wisdom and to the Power which guides and controls the universe.
6. Everyone should follow golden rule of reciprocity. We ought to deal with our fellow beings in the same way as we would like to be dealt with by them in similar situations.
7. Spiritual attainments and advances made through righteous life here are permanently conserved in the spirit.
8. Man is himself is responsible for his fall or progress. It is entirely in the hands of individuals to be where he wishes to be on the scale of being.
9. The root cause of war lies in our wrong outlook of life. Peace is the natural outcome of the right view of ourselves, of our relations to others, and of the values of life.

To quote Gandhiji, "My Hindu instinct tells me that all religions are more or less true. All proceed from the same God, but all are imperfect because they have come down to us through imperfect human instrumentality". Again, "Religions are different roads converging to the same point. What does it matter that we take different roads, so long as we reach the same goal? In reality, there are as many religions as there are individuals". Further he said, "In theory, since there is one God, there can be only one religion. But in practice, no two persons I have known have had the same identical conception of God. Therefore, there will, perhaps, always be different religions answering to different temperaments and climatic conditions".

When Gandhiji speaks of religion, he does not mean any conventional or usual religion, but that religion which is at the root of all religions and that this fundamental religion harmonises the historical religions and makes them valid. Just as a tree has one trunk but many branches and leaves, so there is one true and perfect religion, although it is divided into many, as it appears through a human intermediary. He briefly defines religion as a trust in the moral organisation of the universe. The goal of man's life is to conquer evil in himself and reach the good. Religions are different roads to the same goal. For this, one must not reject other religions, but anybody belonging to any religion can receive from others what is good in them.

Gandhiji's basic motive was purely religious and he could not lead a religious life unless he identified himself with the whole of mankind and he could not do that without participating in politics. He considered religion more important than his country and that he was thus a Hindu first and a nationalist second. Politics is the application of religion to him. His ideas were based upon religious tradition, not political, juridical, philosophical or economic. He always tried to base his political and economic doctrine on religion. His political and economic ideas are to be found in religious tradition. The fact that Gandhiji was a religious reformers means that he had clear, or at least working criteria for right belief. Religion was not for him simply a devout feeling or respect for holy things. On countless occasions, he attacked the exploitation and senselessness which occur in the name of religion.

Gandhiji considered religion to be a very personal matter. It is based upon the individual's own experience ability to understand. He considers it the duty of every civilised man and woman to read with sympathy the writings of every religion. He said, "You must watch my life; how I live, eat, sit, behave in general. The sum total of all these in me is my religion". *Swaraj* is synonymous with *Ramraj*. His aim was to spiritualise politics, economics and society. He believed in absolute oneness of God and therefore also of humanity. He said, "If one gains spiritually, the whole world gains with him, and if one man falls, the whole world falls to that extent".

Gandhiji's religion may be characterised as ethical spiritualism. To him, any religion without a moral foundation ceased to be a religion. Religion and morality are two faces of the same coin wherein neither of them could be separated from each other. He held the view that religion was to morality what water was to the seed sown in the soil. He found the essence of religion in morality or ethics. He said, "To me, God is truth and love; God is ethics and morality; God is fearlessness. God is the source of Light and Life and yet. He is above and beyond, all these. God is conscious. He is even the atheism of atheist". Again, "morals, ethics, and religion are convertible terms. A moral life without reference to religion is like a house built upon sand. And religion divorced from morality is like sounding brass good only for making a noise and breathing heads".

Gandhiji recognised that prayer is the very core of man's life, since it is most significant part of religion. Prayer is a type of inward communication with God leading to the cleansing and purification of the soul by removing the dues of ignorance and darkness which envelop it. Prayer is an effective means to bring to the surface the divine element in every human being.

Service to man is worship of God. Gandhiji said, "The immediate service of all human beings becomes a necessary part of the endeavours, simply because the only way to find God is to see Him in His creation and be one with it". He knew that God is found more often in the lowest of His creatures than in the high and mighty. He knew of no greater sin than to oppress the innocent in the name of God. The only acceptable form in which God can dare appear is work and promise of food as wages. He said, "If any action of mine, claimed to be spiritual, is proved to be impracticable, it must be pronounced to be a failure, I do not believe that the most spiritual act is the most practical in the true sense of the term".

Gandhiji interpreted religion with the day-to-day problems. His mission was not only to humanise religion but also to moralise it. To him, true religion and true morality are inseparably bound with each other. Religion is to morality what water is to the seed that is sown in the soil. There is no religion higher than truth and righteousness. He was of the opinion that as soon as we lose moral basis, we cease to be religious. God can never be realised by one who is not pure at heart. Without self-purification we cannot identify

God. His ultimate aim in equating religion with morality was to make religion dynamically operative in human life. He was quite sure that the biggest challenge to religions was not from the side of atheists but rituals and dogmatists. He wanted to revolutionise politics with ethics, economics with morality and even was with righteousness.

Gandhiji lived in God consciousness, fighting the battle of life. The fullest life is impossible without an immovable belief in a living law in obedience to which the whole universe moves. He calls God as an indefinable mysterious power that pervades everything. He said, "To seek God one need not go on a pilgrimage or light lamps or burns incense before the image of the deity or paint it with red vermilion. For He resides in our hearts, however, we must reduce ourselves to zero to be face to face with God. Hence religion is the pathway to God-realisation. It is human effort to reach God. Scriptures cannot transcend reason and truth. They are intended to purify reason and illuminate truth. He rejected all religious doctrine that does not appeal to reasons. Error can claim no exemption even if it can be supported by the scriptures of the world".

Gandhiji did not believe in people telling others of their faith especially with a view to conversion. He thought that God has created different faiths just as he has the votaries thereof. In God's house, there are many mansions and they are equally holy. He believed in the fundamental truth of all great religions of the world. He preached consistently about the power of truth and *ahimsa* based on the equality of all human beings, the regulations of human desires, the purity of means and ends and simplicity of life. He had a dynamic concept of religion with its essence to be found in morality and truth. He believed in the fundamental value of all religions which emphasised the absolute value of truth, morality and justice.

Gandhiji said that there could not be any politics without religion and that he entered politics because he was primarily a religious man. He said, "But though by disclaiming sainthood, I disappoint the critics expectations, I would have him give up his regrets by answering him that the politician in me has never dominated a single decision of mine, and if I seek to take part in politics, it is only because politics encircle us today like the coil of a snake from which one cannot get out, no matter how much one tries. I wish, therefore, to wrestle with the snake, as I have been doing with more or less success consciously since 1894, unconsciously, as I have now discovered, ever since, reaching years of discretion. Quite selfishly, as I wish to live in peace in the midst of a bellowing storm howling round me, I have been experimenting with myself and friends by introducing religion into politics".

Gandhiji believed that a religious individual could overcome the savage instinct in man and substituting in its place human capacity for good and noble deeds. He introduced religion into politics by identifying himself with service to humanity. He said, "Politics bereft of religion are absolute dirt ever to be shunned. Politics concern nations and that which concern the welfare of nations must be one of the concerns of a man who is religiously inclined, in other words, a seeker after God and truth . . . therefore in politics also we have to establish the Kingdom of Heaven".

Gandhiji believed that even in the political sphere religion had a specific role to play. He was of the opinion that the religious men were politicians in disguise. Ethical values like humanity, forgiveness, tolerance, etc., which were intrinsic to every religion were good antidote to the arrogance of power-hungry politicians. He said, "For me, the road to salvation lies through incessant toil in the service of my country and humanity. I want to identify myself with everything that lives. In the language of the *Gita*, I want to live at peace with both friend and foe. So my patriotism is, for me, a stage on my journey to the land of eternal freedom and peace. Thus, it will be seen that for me there are no politics devoid of religion. They subserve religion. Politics bereft of religion are a death-trap because they kill the soul".

Gandhiji felt that a religious motive was in tune with an individual's desire to take part in politics. There was no question of dividing social, political and religious dimensions into watertight compartments. He took an enlightened view of religion whose objective was to popularise progressive social, political and economic ideas. To him, any religion that gave sanction to antiquated and repressive social custom and tyrannical political authority was the negation of true religion.

Gandhiji considered all castes and communities as equal. He was secular in the sense that he was against coercion to seek conformity to certain creeds. He did not believe in state religion even though the whole community had one religion. He was against the state aid to religious bodies. He distinguished between religion and ethics. He regarded religion as a private matter but the teachings of ethics were certainly a major concern of the state. Religion was essential to prescribe norms and values in politics as it regulated the political activities of politicians as well as the masses. He felt that politics without religion was akin to a life without any principle. He believed in the religious foundation of politics.

Tagore said, "Leave this chanting and singing and telling of beads. Whom dost thou worship in this lonely dark corner of a temple with doors all shut. Open thine eyes and see thy God is not before thee". To quote Swami Vivekanand, "Temples and Churches, books and forms are simply the kindergarten of religion, to make the spiritual child strong enough to take higher steps. Religion is not in doctrines, in dogmas, nor in intellectual argumentation; it is being and becoming, and it is realisation".

Gandhiji's religion is not the religion of merely uttering the name of God. To him, religion is not pride, pedantry or sophistry. He did not mean this or that religion, a denominational faith, or a creed or a sect. His religion is the science of soul and God. Religion is a friend of liberation and a foe to fanaticism. He was of the opinion that religion means recognising the self, recognition of the cosmic life, recognition of Reality, seeing God face to face, attaining *Mokaha* through service to man. God and man are not two independent entities. Religion binds man to God and man to man.

Gandhiji's religion lays stress in morality. His religion can be said to be the synthesis of the three *yogas—Bhakti*, *Jnana* and *Karma*. His religion includes all faiths in the world. He said, "In spite of my being a staunch Hindu, I find room in my faith for Christian and Islamic and Zoroastrian teaching, and, therefore, my Hinduism seems to some to be a conglomeration and some have even dubbed me an eclectic. Well, to call a man eclectic is to say that he has no faith, but mine is a broad faith which does not oppose Christians—not even a plymouth brother—not even the most fanatical Mosalman. It is that broad faith that sustains me. It is a somewhat embarrassing position, I know—but to others, not to me". His religion includes the idea of unity in the world.

In his lifetime, Gandhiji was variously labelled, a Sanatanist Hindu, a renegade Hindu, a Buddhist, a Theosophist, a Christian and a Christian-Mohammadan. He was all these and more. His advocacy of mutual toleration and respect between different religions originally arose from his study of comparative religion, but it had a practical aspect too. In 1934, Albert Einstein said that the more profound scientists were not without a religious feeling though it was different from the religiosity of the common man.

Gandhiji believes in the equality of the principal religions of the world. He prefers it to call it as equality of all religions to tolerance of all religions. We should not consider other religious beliefs as inferior to our own. We have to give respect to all religions. To him, the different religions were beautiful flowers from the same garden or branches of the same majestic tree. All religions were at the bottom one and were all helpful to one another. He held all religions were equally true. Each one of the religions embodies a common motivating force—the desire to uplift man's life and give it a purpose. Men being imperfect, all religions are also imperfect revelations of truth and liable to error. Thus there is no religion that is absolutely perfect. All are equally imperfect or more or less perfect. He was not in favour of conversion from one religion to another. He felt that all religions were equally glorious and that those who were born Hindus need not search for truth in other religions.

A *satyagrahi* should honour and study all religions. The study will help him to grasp the basic unity of all religions and to cultivate equimindedness towards them. Acceptance of equality of religions necessarily prevents proselytising. The *satyagrahi* should not have even a secret wish in his mind that other people should be converted to his faith. Equal respect for religions, however, does not mean toleration of irreligion or being blind to the faults of other faiths. No single religion can claim to be perfect. Everybody is right from his own standpoint, but it is not impossible that everybody is wrong. In each religion, we could see the same fundamental morality.

The acceptance of the doctrine of equality of religions does not abolish the distinction between religion or irreligion. We do not propose to cultivate toleration for irreligion. We have to respect the basic teachings of all religious faiths equally, but to give due value to each other's religion of sentiments. The seekers of Truth should have an equal vision of all religions. If we follow the law of love, we shall not bear any hatred towards the irreligious brother.

Gandhiji subscribed to the creed of equal regard for all faiths and creeds—*Sarvadharma Samanatva*. But he made it clear that equal regard did not mean that one should adopt the other's religion. It only meant understanding the viewpoint of others while adhering to one's own point of view. It meant emphasising the point of agreement and not the point of difference. He was a Hindu himself and admired it for its unique characteristics. But Hinduism to him was not limited to eating and not-eating, it did not consist of ritualism and dogma. He considered Hinduism as the most tolerant creed because it succeeded in absorbing even creeds opposed to it like Buddhism. He said, "Hinduism is not an exclusive religion. In it, there is room for the worship of all the prophets of the world. It is not a missionary religion in the ordinary sense of the term. Hinduism tells everyone to worship God according to his own faith or *dharma*, and so it lives at peace with all religions". He considered Hinduism not a mere religion but a way of life, relentless pursuit of Truth. It was his Hindu instinct which led him to understand the real spirit behind different religions.

Gandhiji was not religious in the ordinary sense in which religion is understood in India. It was religion based on truth and non-violence. That is why religion for him became the basis of all his activities, it became his philosophy of life, it functioned as a source of strength in him. He made it clear that religion in its real sense could become the basis of friendship among all mankind. On the basis of his own experience, he came to the conclusion that all religions were true and based on the same principles of truth and non-violence. He emphasised repeatedly that religions were not for separating men from one another but rather for binding them. He was pained to see the conflict between different religions, he suffered personally to establish harmony and as a matter of fact laid down his life for the cause of religious unity.

According to Gandhiji, the aim of religion was to lead man face to face with God. He considered God as identical to Truth. He tried to see God through the service of humanity, because he knew that God did not live in some far off place in heaven but in the heart of every one of His creations. As God has created different faiths, there could be no question of our having only one religion. He said, "Man's ultimate aim is the realisation of God, and all his activities, political, social and religious have to be guided by the ultimate aim of the vision of God. The immediate service of all human beings becomes a necessary part of the endeavour simply because the only way to find God is to see Him in His creation and be one with it. This can be done by service of all". Again, "If I could persuade myself that I should find Him in a Himalayan cave I would proceed there immediately. But I know that I cannot find Him apart from humanity".

Gandhiji's faith in God was like that of an *Advaitin*. But at the same time, he called himself an *anekant avadin* or believer in the relativity of Reality. His support to two different ideas of reality helped him in correctly judging different religions. It was this balanced religious approach which led him to take the whole world in the embrace of his love. Truth and non-violence are the two principles which could help him in evolving a comprehensive view of religion above narrow sectarianism. For him there was no higher way of worshipping God than serving the poor and identifying himself with them.

According to Gandhiji, the nearest approach to Truth or God was through love of mankind. He took love in the sense of non-violence. It was on this understanding that he tried to explain that differences in religions were only in their methods of approach to God. Everyone of us must identify oneself with other human beings because God is within us. Truth and love are the instruments which bind us to one another and to God. As a Hindu, he did not believe in the orthodox view of God and had no faith in idol worship.

Gandhiji laid emphasis on the three cardinal virtues of really religious person—first truth as divine quality; second, non-violence and third *brahmacharya*. He considered non-violence as the supreme religious duty in accordance with the teachings of the *Mahabharata*. Non-violence is the basis of sympathy with all creeds and kindness. If one does not believe in non-violence he has no kindness for others. Thus sympathy and kindness towards all men becomes the basis of true religion. He used to stress this point in his post-prayer addresses and often quoted the sage and poet Tulsidas in this connection. Thus religion for him did not consist of worshipping God or reading a religious book, it consisted of entire human activity. He regarded religion as self-realisation, as the striving of the human personality to express itself in service, suffering and sacrifice.

Through the religious principles of truth and love, Gandhiji wanted to create a social order devoid of classes and castes. He described himself as a social revolutionist. At the age of twelve, he came to understand that the concept of untouchability was against the real spirit of Hindu religion and was a sin. He made a thorough study of the Hindu scriptures and came to the conclusion that regarding certain people as untouchables was not only against reason but also against the real spirit of Hindu religion. He considered untouchability as something against the instinct of mercy, pity and love. A religion believing in the worship of cow could not possibly recommend boycott of human beings, the suppressed classes. In the eyes of God all creatures are equal. God had endowed all human beings impartially with the same shape and the same natural desires. Therefore, there could never be a religious sanction to look down upon any human being as inferior to us.

Hinduism and Gandhiji

Gandhiji develops his religious thought in the background of Hinduism. He is a theist who believes in one God as the creator, maintainer and destroyer of the universe. His philosophy of God as Truth expands and universalises his religious faith. He believes in the existence of self and rebirth based on the principles of *Karma*. He accepts the Hindu view of the incarnation of God in human form to overpower evil and to establish the forces of goodness in the society. He revives truth, non-violence, renunciation, celibacy, etc., for the spiritualisation of mankind. He subscribes to the principles of *Varnashrama* and considers it to be a good system of society. Men should adopt professions on the basis of their heredity and training. Everyone should divide one's life into four stages or *asramas*.

Gandhiji calls himself as a Sanatani Hindu, because of the following:

1. He believes in the *Vedas*, the *Upanishads*, the *Puranas* and all that goes by the name of Hindu scriptures, and therefore in *avatars* and rebirth;
2. He believes in the *Varnashrama Dharma* in a sense, in his opinion, strictly vedic, but not in its present popular and crude sense;
3. He believes in the protection of cow in its much larger sense than the popular; and
4. He does not disbelieve in idol worship.

Gandhiji accepts Hindu scriptures to the extent they are rational and based on truth. For him the *Vedas* and the *Upanishads* are not the only revealed scriptures. The teachings of the Hindu scriptures have to be tested in the light of truth. Nehru said, "claiming to understand the spirit of Hinduism, he rejects every text or practice which does not fit in with his idealistic interpretation of what it should be, calling it an interpolation or a subsequent accretion".

God incarnates Himself in human form to save the righteous persons and destroy the unrighteous ones. Hinduism is full of such incarnations. Gandhiji subscribes that human body which is in bondage undergoes several births till it reaches the highest state of perfection. He was against the caste system in India. The caste system is a drag upon the progress of humanity for it unnecessarily emphasises restrictions on inter-dining and inter-marriage, divisions and sub-divisions, and the notions of superiority and inferiority.

Gandhiji defends the original conception of *Varna* because it is based on spiritual economy, division of labour, and equality of man. He removes the idea of superiority and inferiority of man belonging to the different *varnas*. All men are equal. God is present in it. So, all professions stand on equal footing. He holds that *Varnashrama* brings the greatest communism on earth. He said, "I am inclined to think that the law of heredity is an eternal law, and that any attempt to alter it must lead to utter confusion. *Varnashrama*, or the caste system, is inherent in human nature. Hinduism has simply reduced it to a science".

Cow-protection is the central principle of Hinduism. To Gandhiji, cow is the symbol of the entire sub-human world. He condemns the fetishism of the so-called believers who observes the letter of cow-worship without having compassion for the dump creatures of the world. He lays stress on cow-protection. To quote Romain Rolland, "Whoever understands the spirit of compassion and fellow-feeling that Gandhi would have men feel for their dumb brethren is not surprised that Gandhi lays such stress on cow-protection in his creed. From this point of view, he is quite justified in saying that cow-protection is the gift of Hinduism to the world".

Gandhiji favours image worship for those persons who are unable to concentrate their minds on God without His concrete symbols. The external worship is the lowest stage, mental prayer is the next, but the highest stage is one of following with God. The external performance of religion is necessary only at the initial stages. The dogmas, rituals, images and sacraments initiate a man and make him God-conscious. He said, "I do not regard the existence of a temple as a sin or superstition. Some form of common worship, and a common place of worship appear to be a human necessity. Whether the temples should contain images or not is a matter of temperament and taste".

Gandhiji is not the author of a new religion nor does he want to see that his conception of religion becomes a sect in Hinduism. Religion should pervade everyone of our actions. Here religion does not mean sectarianism. His broad conception of religion leaves no room for founding a new religion or a sect. He claims to represent the old truth. To quote D.S. Sharma, "The people knew that he always meant what he said, that he practised what he preached, and that he was far more severe on himself than others. They knew that he was not simply a political leader or a social reformer or a friend of the poor, but, first and foremost, a man of God, a saint and a *sannyasin* after their own heart. He represented what every Hindu admired and tried to be, but could not achieve. Renunciation, self-control and penance have been the cherished ideals of Hindus from time immemorial and here was a man who was an embodiment of those ancient virtues and who combined with them the most far-sighted statesmanship, the widest toleration and the tenderest love. No wonder, therefore, that the Hindus of the present day look upon him as the true descendant of their ancient *Risis*, reinterpreting their *Sanatana Dharma* according to the needs of the present age and giving them a new code of conduct".

In Hinduism we find a number of mystics who withdraw from the world, contemplate on God and realise union with Him. Gandhiji's mysticism is the mysticism of perfection through action. Without liberating the imperfect humanity no single individual can attain salvation. He has achieved spiritual communion with God. He believes in the existence of God. He said, "I do have a living faith in a living God even as I have a living faith in many things that scientists tell me". God reveals Himself in many ways. He marches from one stage of spiritual progress to the other. He receives the message of God. He said, "I have been a willing slave to this most exacting Master for more than half a century. His voice has been increasingly audible as years have rolled by. He has never forsaken me even in my darkest hour. The greater the surrender to Him, the greater has been my joy". He alludes to his experience of the presence of God. It is his feeling of the supreme spirit everywhere. His life is a guided life in the sense that he has communed with his inner spirit and has done the bidding that came. He heard the commanding Voice which gave him clear and definite instructions and responded to questions asked by him.

Gandhiji's mysticism is not based on negative principle. He wants to free himself from the fetters of flesh but for this he is not prepared to accept the old Hindu ideal of withdrawal from the world. His mysticism is the mysticism of perfection through action. This is his distinct contribution to Hinduism. He removes two main misconceived ideas form the minds of the Hindus. One of the ideas nurtured in the Hindu minds is that action leads one to suffer its evil consequences. Everyone believes that one suffers for the evils committed by him. He observes that the view resulted in unhealthy attitude of men towards the social problems of the world.

There were upper castes and lower castes in Hinduism which further were divided into touchables and untouchables. Temples were not open to all. The *Vedas* were the exclusive monopoly of the Brahmins. Knowledge of the Hindu scriptures was denied to the people other than Brahmins. This resulted in their ignorance which ultimately affected the development of the people. Conservatism had overpowered the Hindus. Moral and religious values became decadent. An ugly and unhealthy practice that we find in Hinduism is the indulgence in communal disharmony and conversion or reconversion by force. This has narrowed the broad outlook of tolerance in Hinduism.

A section of Hindus is regarded as 'Untouchables'. They cannot move, mix and unite with caste Hindus. Gandhiji said, "I regard untouchability as the greatest blot on Hinduism". Again, "There was a time when I was wavering between Hinduism and Christianity. When I recovered my balance of mind, I felt that to me salvation was possible only through the Hindu religion and my faith in Hinduism grew deeper and more enlightened. But even then I believed that untouchability was no part of Hinduism; and that, if it was, such Hinduism was not for me'. He is not working for removing the system of untouchables in their houses and lives in the colonies of Harijans. In his own *ashram* he arranges so many marriages which necessarily include Harijans. He may be regarded as the saviour of Hinduism. His idealism has been expressed in the following lines—In the purest type of Hinduism, an ant, an elephant and a dog-eater are of the same status. Hinduism insists on the brotherhood not only of all mankind but of all the lives.

Gandhiji accords equal reverence to other faiths as for one's own. He treats persons of different religions on a footing of equality. It is the duty of the Hindus to behave well towards others and only then can expect similar behaviour from them. Conflict arises when there is a feeling of assuming one's religion as superior and other religions as inferior. It is in Hinduism that there is a room for the worship of all the prophets in the world. His contribution to Hinduism remains unsurpassed in so far as his spirit and efforts for tolerance in Hinduism are concerned. His life is a clear demonstration of the fact that the Hindus can live harmoniously with the non-Hindus.

Gandhiji tries to evolve a cultless, non-credal, non-dogmatic and non-ritualistic form of Hinduism. He universalises Hinduism by removing its limitations, boundaries and elements which make it closed and static. To him, Hinduism is a dynamic, open, universal, creative and evolving religion which ever enriches itself by assimilation of truths. He wants to break all barriers between religions and remove all conflicts and oppositions. He wants diversity in religions which reveal spiritual awakening and evolution of humanity. The different religions are necessary because they emphasise the different aspects of Truth. Hinduism derives truth from the mystic experiences of the seers. It accepts all religions to be true. It is an all-comprehensive religion. He simplifies Hinduism and infuses practical idealism in it.

5

ON STATELESS SOCIETY

Gandhiji was not an inspired political philosopher destined to propound a new political philosophy and contemplate the world in the light of his creative vision. He was a great leader of Indian national liberation movement, who humbled the mighty British imperialism. He proposed alternatives in almost all areas of human life and activity and strove to device effective strategies for realisation of the goal of human life as he conceived it. He was not a model-builder. He was not concerned with consistency; rather he was concerned with the truth as perceived from time to time. He was not a theorist or a visionary, but a practical idealist, a man of action who incessantly experimented with the Truth, who continued to learn and evolve. He appears differently to different persons.

Though not a political scientist in its rigid sense, Gandhiji was such a supreme thinker and reformer who had very consistent and clear conception of the State as it should be, and defined the nature and structure of political institutions. The basis of Gandhian State is the active cooperation of the people. The social structure of Gandhian State is founded on the moral ideal of self-realisation which inspires and moulds the conception of life in all spheres. He believed that he was experimenting with truth and 'as a seeker after truth he had a firm faith in a good deed producing a good result. He must live and act in the present dealing with problems as they arise, concentrating on the immediate duties without attachment to the fruits thereof'. He had a living faith in the Divine Government and believed that even a blade of grass does not but move by His will. He thought that he was merely an agent of God and was carrying out His will.

Gandhiji did not put forward any theory about the genesis of the State. He said, "The State evil is not the cause but the effect of social evil; just as the sea-waves are the effect, nor the cause of storm". In the past, we find city republics in Greece and India. Later on, these were changed into monarchy and finally into democracy. The king was the head in monarchy. The Greek philosophers believed that the State contributed in greater degree than any other social institution, to the realisation of the finer and nobler capacities of man. Plato was of the opinion that education to be the true function of the State and insisted that the State, albeit in its ideal form, makes the man.

In the West, there are two view-points about the State. One view was that the State is an organism of which men themselves are parts, and which, therefore, is greater than them. The State is real and the individual is merely an abstraction. The other view was that the State is but a machine, a device, designed by men for their own purposes. The former view was developed by the Greeks. In the 17th century, this was challenged and gave birth to latter view. This view was again challenged in the 18th century. But, both views still persist. Rousseau considers the State as a collective person, an embodiment of the General Will; but he also considers the State as an association formed by men for their own purposes. From both these angles, obedience to the State becomes imperative. Hegel regarded the State as omnipotent, infallible, absolute, the perfected rationality, the crystallisation of morality.

Till the end of the Middle ages, the State had played only a limited role. There were several constraints on the operation of the dynamics of power. Industrial revolution changed the face of the world. The system of capitalism arose. Development of capitalism led to the atomisation of society. The rural social structure that had developed around the nucleus of agriculture gave way under the grinding force of industrialism. The community was destroyed and the society was converted into an amorphous mass. The historical situation transformed the State qualitatively and the modern State was born.

The State alienated from society. To quote Erich Fromn, "Man submits to the State as to the embodiment of his own social feelings, which he worships as powers alienated from himself; in his private life as an individual he suffers from the isolation and aloneness which are the necessary result of this separation". Again, "The worship of the State can only disappear if man takes back the social powers into himself and builds a community in which his private and social existence are one and the same". The State weakened and almost displaced other associations gradually. The industrial growth which caused the birth of the modern State also caused one more development. The technological growth placed immense power in the hands of the Western States. This gave rise to imperialism and colonialism.

Gandhiji understood the role of capitalism in the emergence of the modern State as an omnipotent supreme authority. He said, "capitalism has, by making State intervention necessary in economic affairs, contributed to the emergence of all-powerful State which makes individual freedom impossible and is the greatest danger the world faces. The real problem today is to devise checks and balances on such a State and to prevent its rise".

Marxism believes in the withering away of the State. The Marxian view regarding the State can be summarised from Engel's passage, "The State is, therefore, by no means a power forced on society from without; just as little is it the reality of the ethical idea, the image and reality of reason as Hegal maintains. Rather, it is a product of society at a certain stage of development, it is the admission that this society has become entangled in an insoluble contradiction with itself, that it has split into irreconcilable antagonisms which it is powerless to dispel. But in order that these antagonisms, these classes with conflicting economic interests might not consume themselves and society in fruitless struggle, it became necessary to have a power, seemingly standing above society, that would alleviate the conflict and keep it within the bounds of order; and this power arisen out of society but placing itself above it, and alienating itself more and more from it, is the State".

In the Marxist conception, a State is essentially a 'Class State'. According to this view, a State is ultimately governed by those elements and interests in society that are economically the most powerful. Those who control the economic power ultimately decide the character of the State, whatever may be the outward form. Marx and Engel's views regarding the State are complex and in many ways contradictory. Marxists believed in the withering away of the States; not its abolition. Marx had hailed the Paris commune as the finally discovered political form which was to be the political form of even the smallest village. Engel was of the opinion that the seizure of the means of production would be the last independent act of the proletarian State, as a State. The ambiguity in the Marx's and Engel's thought helped the Leninistic interpretation gain acceptance in the Communist movement.

Pierre Joseph Proudhan believed in a genuine and radical reconstruction of society. He denounced centralisation and remarked that the limitations of the State's task is a matter of life and death for freedom, both collective and individual. He was a federalist. He recognised that the real problem to be solved for federalism is not political, but economic and hence proposed mutualism. He called property 'theft' and saw the State as evolving out of the system of private property and as sustainer of that system. He, therefore, proposed a national exchange bank to eliminate private capital. He advocated a political structure based on decentralisation.

Prince Peter Kropotkin saw State as an historical growth that displaces free communities at a certain stage in history. He stressed that the law of organic evolution is primarily a law of mutual aid; not of conflict. Individuals and species that survive are those endowed with the most effective faculties for cooperation in the struggle to adopt themselves to their environment; those in which the competitive qualities are more predominant disappear eventually. He said, "A society of mutual insurance between the landlord, the military commander, the judge, the priest and the capitalist in order to support each other's authority over the people and for exploiting the poverty of the masses and getting rich themselves".

Leo Tolstoy's doctrine has been called Christian anarchism. To him, the State, private property and organised churches were incompatible with Christianity. He said, "Since the State and the class hierarchy are evil, the disciple of Jesus must be a rebel, a conscientious objector". He did not speculate on the future organisations of society. He considered it neither possible nor necessary. He advocated non-violence, bread labour, simplicity and passive resistance to all evils.

Since State is deeply rooted in violence and perpetuates exploitation, Gandhiji stood for its abolition. It has no place in a perfectly non-violent set-up of society. He condemns State not so much that it is an agency of domination but more due to the fact that it checks the ethical and moral development of man. Thus the State corrupts the thinking of man, demoralises them and leaves them into a state of object surrender. He viewed State as opposed to the nature of man. He defined man in certain moral and spiritual terms. Man is not merely a mass of bones and flesh but something more. There is also a spirit, a soul in him which is, though invisible but is all pervading and self-conscious and is a part and parcel of God. The fundamental urge of man is for freedom, peace and happiness. He said, "The individual has a soul and the State soulless, it can never be weaned from violence to which it owes its very existence". The individual of Gandhiji is a master of himself, of his thoughts, intentions, deeds and passions. He is answerable to none but to himself, for he has acquired his bestself and reached a higher stage. When society is composed of such individuals, there is no place for the mechanism of State. State retards the growth of individual's personality and is destructive to his freedom. So he views every increase in the powers of the State with fear.

Gandhiji characterised the State as an embodiment of violence and a soulless machine. He said, "I look upon an increase in the power of the State with the greatest fear because, although while apparently doing good by minimising exploitation, it does the greatest harm by destroying individuality which lies at the root of all progress". The State only apparently minimises exploitation. In fact, exploitation is the essence of violence and the State is the embodiment of violence. He said, "We know of so many cases where men have adopted trusteeship, but none where the State has really lived for the poor". He was of the opinion that the violence of private ownership is less injurious than the violence of the State. His objection to the State mainly can be seen on three grounds : (1) It is an embodiment of violence, (2) It is soulless and (3) It destroys individuality and hence retards progress.

Gandhiji saw State basically as an organisation of violence. That the ultimate sanction of the State is coercion and violence has not been denied, although it is considered necessary for its legitimacy that it has consent of a large body of the governed. That consent does mean that the violence employed by the State is qualitatively different, and later Vinoba did distinguish between *Hinashakti* (violence) and *Dandashakti* (coercion employed by the State). Gandhiji disapproved of any organisation based on force and the State is essentially such an organisation.

Gandhiji gave much importance to individual. He said, "Individual is one Supreme consideration". He is an end in himself and the State acts just as a vehicle in and through which the individual realises his best self. He considered individual as an architect of his own government. Individual freedom should be guarded at any cost. He observed that a mean has to be struck between individual freedomand social restraint. He said, "I value individual freedom but you must not forget. . . . Unrestricted individualism is the law of the beast. We have to learn to strike the mean between individual freedom and social restraints". Individual freedom is the prerequisite for man's devotion to social service. He said, "Individual freedom alone can make a man voluntarily surrender himself completely to the service of society.

If it is wrested from him, he becomes an automation and society is ruined. No society can possibly be built on a denial of individual freedom".

Individual interests are not different from society's interest. Only by serving society can he serve himself and serve the God. But this should be voluntary, for "no action, which is voluntary, can be called moral. So long as we act like machines, there can be no question of morality. If we want to call an action moral, it should have been done consciously and as a matter of duty". Gandhiji held that the State is a bondage, a cage to the moral well-being of man. He said, "It is contrary to our manhood if we obey laws repugnant to our conscience. . . . A man who has realised his manhood, who fears only God, will fear no one else. Man-made laws are not necessarily binding on him. . . . We are sunk so low that we fancy that it is our duty and our religion to do what the law lays down. If man will only realise that it is unmanly to obey laws that are unjust, no man's tyranny will enslave him. This is the key to self-rule".

Man should obey the God only. The State, however, demands complete, unflinching and unconditional obedience. Gandhiji believed in the sovereignty of the people, and that too, on the basis of pure moral authority. He would allow obedience to the State-made laws only when they do not offend conscience. To him, disobedience to the law of the State becomes peremptory duty when it comes in conflict with the law of the God. The State is soulless, mechanical and rigid.

The important function of the State is to solve the conflicts in the society and the regulation of social life through law. Gandhiji would have agreed with Godwin that legislation aggravates the natural inequality of man. He attacked the legal system in *Hindu-Swaraj*. He said, "My firm opinion is that the lawyers have enslaved India, have accentuated Hindu-Mahomeadan dissensions and have confirmed English authority". Again, "All I am concerned with is to so that the profession teaches immorality; it is exposed to temptations from which few are saved". The lawyers are not concerned with the dispensation of justice. The lawyers greed for money and their incitement to disputes were objectionable factors for him. He said, "Moreover, men take up that profession, not in order to help others out of their miseries, but to enrich themselves. It is one of the avenues of becoming wealthy and their interest exists in multiplying disputes. It is within my knowledge that they are glad when men have disputes. Petty pleaders actually manufacture them. Their touts, like so many leeches, suck the blood of the poor people". He remarked that the law courts are an essential medium for British rule and those who want to perpetrate their power do so through the courts. He was of the opinion that men were less unmanly when they settled their disputes either by fighting or by asking their relatives to decide for them. He asserted that if people were to settle their own quarrels, a third party would not be able to exercise authority over them.

MacIver agrees that the State's essential instrument, the law, is too general, too clumsy, too formal to touch the essentials of conduct. He remarked, "A legal judgement is a disturbing influence. It operates as an external force. The forms of satisfaction which it offers, through the imposition of damages, through forced sales, injunctions and so forth, bring an alien and abrupt pressure into the established orders of business. If the disputes can get together and settle by their own machinery, their differences, the result is not only less costly but also less disturbing". To quote Jawaharlal Nehru, "Hindu law itself is largely based on custom and customs change and grow. This elasticity of the Hindu law disappeared under the British and gave place to rigid legal codes drawn up after consultation with the most orthodox people. Thus the growth of Hindu society, slow as it was, was stopped".

The State in fact, perpetuates conflicts rather than solving them. Gandhiji would have agreed with Laudauer that the degree of necessity and hence legitimacy of the State is defined by the degree of incapacity of people to regulate their own affairs. This degree should be reduced. The State usually oversteps its limits on account of the operation of the dynamics of power. So there is always the possibility that it may use too much violence against those who differ from it.

Gandhiji agreed that certain things cannot be done without the use of political power. He said, "To me, political power is not an end but one of the means of enabling the people to better their condition in every department of life. Political power is the capacity to regulate national life through national representatives. If national life becomes so perfect as to be self-regulated, no representation becomes necessary. There is then a state of enlightened anarchy". To quote Burckhardt, "Power is of nature evil, whoever wields it. It is not stability, but a lust; and *ipso facto*, insatiable; therefore unhappy in itself and doomed to make others unhappy". Leo Tolstoy held that it is sinful to wield political power, as it leads to many of the evils in the world. Prince Kropotkin was of the opinion that "the absolute power is bound to corrupt even the best amongst us, as they too are not totally perfect". Vinoba said, "The seat of power casts a magic spell over those who occupy it. If instead of those at present occupying it, we were to occupy it, we would do things very similiar to what they are doing".

Gandhiji clearly understood the dynamics of power. He held that a man who wants to be good and do good in all circumstances must not hold power. Herbert Read observed, "Unless society can renounce power and the deliberate actions which arise from the desire to exercise power, there is no escape from the insanity of history. A power structure is the form taken by the inhibition of creativity; the exercise of power is the denial of spontaneity. The will to power, an emotional complex in individuals, directly conflicts with the will to mutuality, which, as Kropotkin showed, is a social instinct".

Democracy is the most predominant form of the modern State. There is hardly any State today, that is undemocratic. In *Hind Swaraj*, Gandhiji attacked the parliamentary system in the strongest words. He called the mother of Parliaments a sterile woman and a prostitute. He said, "We have been long accustomed to think that power comes through legislative assemblies. I have regarded this belief as a grave error brought about by my inertia or hypnotism. A superficial study of the British History has made us think that all power percolates to the people from parliaments. The truth is that power resides in the people and it is entrusted for the time being to those whom they may choose as their representatives. Parliaments have no power or even existence independently of the people. It has been my effort for the last twenty-one years to convince the people of this simple truth". Democratic government is a distant dream so long as non-violence is not recognised as a living force, an inviolable creed, not a mere policy. He rejected majoritarianism. The rule of majority has a narrow application. The rule of majority does not mean that it should suppress the opinion of even an individual, if it is sound. An individual's opinion should have greater weight than the opinion of many, if that opinion is sound on merits. That is his view of real democracy.

Gandhiji defined democracy. He said, "Democracy must . . . mean the art and science of mobilising the entire physical, economic and spiritual resources of all the various sections of the people in the service of the common good of all". The present day democracy fails to do this. His critique of Western-model democracy is prophetic. He said, "corruption is the bane of government by majority". Vinoba has called the real democracy of Gandhiji's conception as *Sarvayatan*. Thus he unequivocally rejected the organic view of the State.

Gandhiji used the term *Ram Rajya* to describe the ideal society of his conception. He put forth the ideal of a Stateless society. He said, "If national life becomes so perfect as to become self-regulated, no representation becomes necessary. There is then a state of enlightened anarchy. In such a state, everyone is his own ruler. He rules himself in such a manner that he is never a hindrance to his neighbour. In the ideal State, therefore, there is no political power because there is no state". He was a *Karmayogi*. He knew that the ideal is never fully realised in life. Hence the classical statement of Thoreau that government is best which governs the least.

According to Gandhiji, "By a non-violent State we mean the State that is predominantly non-violent. A State depending as it does more or less on coercion is the negation of non-violence. The completely non-violent State would no longer be a State. It would then be a Stateless society and society can be Stateless when it is completely or almost completely non-violent. This is an ideal that may not be fully realised. What we may get in actual practice may be predominantly non-violent State advancing towards, though perhaps never reaching, the Stateless stage". Again, "A government cannot succeed in becoming entirely non-violent, because it represents all the people. I do not conceive of such a golden age. But I do believe in the possibility of predominantly non-violent society. And I am working for it". He proposed a predominantly non-violent, more genuinely domocratic system of village republics as an intermediate, realisable goal. At the same time, he worked for a parliamentary form of democratic government which the people desired, as an immediate goal to be achieved by briving out the British rule.

Gandhiji believed that we must have a proper picture of what we want, before we can have something approaching it. He also believed that God has given us only a limited sphere of action and a limited vision; and so one should take care of the present, take care of means, and the end will take care of itself. The means are end-creating. He said, "I have purposely refrained from dealing with the nature of government in a society . . . constructed in accordance with the laws of non-violence, its structure will be different in material particulars from what it is today. But I cannot say in advance what the government based wholly on non-violence will be like".

Gandhiji concerned himself principally with the conservation of the means and their progressive use. He likened the ultimate ideal to the Euclid's definition of a point. He observed, "Theory and practice hardly ever coincide even as Euclid's line in practice never coincides with his theoretical definition". To quote K.G. Mashruwala, "the ideal is like a high peak of the Himalayas. When we perceive it from a distance, we do not realise that it might be too difficult to reach. But as we begin to climb, we find that what we thought to be the final goal is but a stage in the way; and a new far-away mount appears before the vision, as the final one; and this process might take place endlessly".

Gandhiji's ultimate ideal is *Ram Rajya*. By *Ram Rajya*, he meant an ideal society in all respects. He explained *Ram Rajya*. He said, "It can be religiously translated as Kingdom of God on Earth; politically translated it is perfect democracy in which inequalities based on possession and non-possession, colour, race or creed or sex vanish. In it, land and State belong to the people; justice is prompt, perfect and cheap, and therefore, there is freedom of worship, speech and the press—all this because of the reign of the self imposed law of moral restraint. Such a State must be based on Truth and non-violence, and must consist of prosperous, happy and self-contained villages and village communities". There is sovereignty of people based on pure moral authority. He said, "My conception of *Ram Rajya* excludes the replacement of the British army by a national army of occupation. A country that is governed by even its national army can never be morally free and, therefore, its so-called weakest member can never rise to his fullest moral height". *Ram Rajya* denoted an egalitarian, non-violent, self-regulated, democratic order with moral values reigning supreme.

Gandhiji wanted maximisation of self-rule. His concept of *Swaraj* was radically different from the general understanding of the term in his time. To him, mere deliverance from the subjection of an alien power did not mean *Swaraj*. He remarked, "You want the tiger's nature, but not the tiger; that is to say you would make India English. And when it becomes English, it will be called not Hindustan, but Englishtan. This is not the *Swaraj* that I want". Again, "Mere withdrawal of the English is not independence. It means the consciousness in the average villager that he is the maker of his own distiny; he is his own legislator through his chosen representatives'. He said, "No mere transference of political power in India will satisfy my ambition, even though I hold such transference to be a vital necessity of Indian national life". To him, self-government means continuous effort to the independent of governmental control, whether it is a foreign government or whether it is national.

Gandhiji distinguished *Swaraj* from Independence. He explained, "The word *Swaraj* is a scared word, a vedic word, meaning self-rule and self-restraint, and not freedom from all restraint which independence often means". He said, "*Swaraj* of a people menas the sum total of the *Swaraj* (self-rule) of individuals". Further he said, "*Swaraj* government will be a sorry affair if people look up to it for the regulation of every detail of life". He often used the words *Ram Rajya*, *Swaraj* and Independence to mean the same thing. These can be taken as his ultimate, intermediate and immediate goals respectively.

Perfect non-violence is impossible to be practised. The Statelessness is realisable to the extent non-violence is realisable; that is to the extent individuals in the society are imbued with non-violence. Gandhiji is not for the abolition of the State; he believes in the withering away of the State. To quote J.D. Sethi, "In the Marxist as much as in the Gandhian view, the State represents the highest degree of concentration of power and violence. But whereas for one the withering away of the State is the result of violence of one class over another, for the other the power of the State, a necessary evil upto a point, is to be counterbalance by series of institution of a parallel polity". Again he remarked, "For him the role of the State had to be continuously diminished in proportion to the creation of people's institutions of parallel polity, each ultimately acting as a counterbalancing force against the other". To Landauer, State is not an institution. The State is a condition, a certain relationship between human beings, a mode of human behaviour. We destroy it by contracting other relationships, by behaving differently. Non-violence is actually the law of life. The question is to increase the degree of non-violence.

To quote Gandhiji, "Science teaches us that a lever cannot move a body unless it has got a resting body outside the body against which it is applied. Similarly, in order to overcome evil one must stand wholly outside it, that is not the firm solid ground of unadulterated good". The present order can be changed not by directly challenging it; that is unnecessary, unwise and futile. Rather, the people should come together, grow together not in the State; but outside, without a State. Gandhiji was of the opinion that a non-violent revolution is not a programme of transformation of relationships ending in a peaceful experience that if you want something really important to be done, you must not merely satisfy the reason; you must move the heart also. The appeal of reason is more to the head, but the penetration of the heart comes from suffering. It opens up the inner understanding in man. He, therefore, stressed that non-violence in its dynamic condition means conscious suffering.

Political self-government would be feasible in proportion with the individual self-government. Gandhiji said, "But after all self-government depends entirely upon our own internal strength, upon own ability to fight against the heaviest odds. Indeed, self-government which does not require that continuous striving to attain and sustain it is not worth the name. I have therefore endeavoured to show . . . political self-government—that is self-government for a large number of men and women—is no better than individual self-government and therefore it is to be attained by precisely the same means that are required for individual self-government or self-rule". The extent of State power will naturally be related to the internal strength of the people. Gandhiji likened people to the roots and the State to the fruit of a tree.

Vinoba asked, "The government is after all only a bucket, while the people are like a well. If there is no water in the well, how can there be any in the bucket ?" Again he said, "Strength lies with the people in the village. They are all under a false impression that steam power comes from the water contained in the kettle on the stove, whereas steam power is made by the fire burning in the stove, and the water above is simply a passive agent. If there is heat in the stove, then . . . the heat of the villages can make Delhi warm. But what Delhi can do (in return) with regard to the village is like extinguishing that fire".

State being an embodiment of violence cannot be defeated by violence. So Gandhiji repeatedly emphasised that the attainment of *Swaraj* meant cultivation of non-violence. Non-violence does not seek seizure of power; rather it seeks to control and guide power; it humanises it. To qoute Gandhiji, "Real *Swaraj* will come, not by the acquisition of authority by a few, but by the acquisition of the capacity by all to resist authority when it is abused. In other words, *Swaraj* is to be attained by educating the masses to a sense of their capacity to regulate and control authority".

Gandhiji did believe that centralisation is inconsistent with non-violence. And what he essentially wanted was to build a society on non-violence. He therefore believed that if India is to evolve along non-violence lines, it will have to decentralise many things.

He said, "The end to be sought is human happiness combined with full mental and moral growth. I use the adjective moral as synonymous with spiritual. This end can be achieved under decentralisation. Centralisation as a system is in consistent with a non-violent structure of society".

Centralisation cannot be sustained and defended without adequate force. It leads to the concentration of power in a few hands. People are denied any opportunity to participate in their own affairs. When people are not free to shape their own lives and destinies, they cannot feel a sense of involvement in life. Gandhiji condemned urbanisation. He considered it as a factor contributing to exploitation. Urbanisation leads to alienation.

Anarchists, Syndicalists, Guild Socialists, liberal democrats, all plead for the decentralisation of economic and political power. G.D.H. Cole said, "Democracy is hostile to centralisation". C.E.M. Joad observed, "If men's faith in social action is to be revivified, the State must be cut up and its functions distributed. It must be made possible for the individual to belong to a variety of small bodies possessing executive powers, dealing both with production and with local administration, as a member of which he can once again feel that he counts politically, that his will matters'. To quote Aldous Huxley, "the larger a democracy grows, the less real becomes the rule of the people and the smaller is the say of individuals". Bertrand Russell observed, "If concentration of power in a single organisation is not to produce the evils of despotism in an extreme form, it is essential that power within that organisation should be widely distributed, and that subordinate groups should have a large measure of autonomy'.

Saint Simon recognised the significance of the small social unit. Rousseau considered bigness as the enemy of self-government. Tolstoy remarked that going back to the village community was the only solution towards a natural life. Prince Kropotkin pleaded for a decentralised set-up. Herbert Read explained that individual freedom can only be preserved in small communities, free from a central and impersonal exercise of power; communities developing by mutual aid and with complete respect for the personality.

The instinct of mutual aid and cooperation can develop in small communities. To quote Herbert Read, "Conscience itself is born of this relationship, and all those instincts of mutuality and sympathy which become codified. . . . Religion and politics follow, as attempts to define the instinctive conduct natural to the group". A community is born out of a life shared in common. Society is naturally composed, not of atomised individuals, but of communities and the associations between them.

Gandhiji was of the opinion that Society based on non-violence can only consist of groups settled in villages, in which voluntary cooperation is the condition of dignified and peaceful existence. He remarked that the nearest approach to civilisation based upon non-violence is the erstwhile village republic of India. He believed that India is the only country which has a possibility of being a non-violent State. Regarding the decentralisation of politics in India, Dr. Altekar remarked, "The village communities and town councils to a great extent resembled small republics, where the voice of the people . . . advocated and brought about in ancient India was thus the most effective and practical check upon the King's powers". To quote Metcalfe, "They seem to last where. . . .Union of the village communities, each one forming a separate little State . . . is in a high degree conducive to their happiness and to the enjoyment of a great portion of freedom and independence".

R.C. Dutt called the effacement of the system of village self-government as one of the saddest results of British rule in India. Vinoba said, "The country was in subjugation at the time of Moghul emperors, but the villages were independent. Villagers used to look after the village affairs. Later, the British destroyed village industries and village panchayats, resulting in the subjugation of the villages in addition to the country. After India's independence, country is independent, but the villages remain under slavery".

Gandhiji held that real India lives in its villages. He said, "Independence must begin at the bottom. Thus every village will be a republic or panchayat having full powers. It follows, therefore, that every village has to be self-sustained and capable of managing its affairs". He explained the idea of village *Swaraj*. He said, "My idea of village *swaraj* is that it is a complete republic, independent of its neighbours for its vital wants and yet interdependent for many others in which dependence is necessary. . . . The government of the village will be conducted by the Panchayat of five persons, annually elected by the adult villagers, male and female, possessing minimum prescribed qualifications. . . . Here there is perfect democracy based upon individual freedom. The individual is the architect of his own government".

Gandhiji believed in the obedience to moral law. With the cultivaion of non-violence in the society and development of conscience, crime will be reduced. He remarked, "Crime is a disease like any other malady and is a product of the prevalent social system". Again he said, "I have not the courage to declare that we can carry on without a police force as I have in respect of an army. Of course I can and do envisage a State where the police will not be necessary; but whether we shall succeed in realising it, the future alone will show". He explained his ideas of police force. He said, "Its ranks will be composed of believers in non-violence. They will be servants, not masters, of the people. The people will instinctively render them every help, and through mutual cooperation they will easily deal with ever-decreasing . . . the policemen will be reformers. Their police work will be confined primarily to robbers and dacoits".

There is no need for violent army in a non-violent society. Gandhiji said, "A non-violent army acts unlike armed men, as well in times of peace as of disturbances. They would be constantly engaged in constructive activities that make riots impossible. Theirs will be the duty of seeking occasions for bringing warring communities together, carrying on peace propaganda, engaging in activities that would bring and keep them in touch with every single person . . . in order to still the frenzy of mobs, should risk their lives in numbers sufficient for the purpose. A few hundred, may be a few thousand, such spotless deaths will once for all put an end to the riots. Surely a few hundred young men and women giving themselves deliberately to mob fury will be any day a cheap and braver method of dealing with such madness than the display and use of the police and the military".

A non-violent society will not be afraid of any aggression. It will not exploit or deceive anybody. It would strive to settle disputes by peaceful methods. Gandhiji rejected capital punishment, an irrevocable act, asserting that God alone can take life, because He alone gives it.

Gandhiji thus decisively rejected the centralised apparatus of the modern State. He pleaded for a decentralised polity constituting of a federation of autonomous village republics. The village panchayat will look after the vital tasks of education, sanitation, industries, land management, cattle development and the like. Polity will be like the oceanic circles wherein inner circles will have as much effective power as possible. He rejected any justification for the State on account of its supposedly vital functions. Many of its functions are superfluous or inflated; many functions are just pretexts to acquire more powers. Most of the functions of the State can be discharged in a much better way by voluntary associations and primary communities. People should have the right and opportunity to shape their destinies. Political power should be a means to achieve this end.

The end to be sought is freedom from the State. It will not be achieved immediately. Achievement of this ideal will be a continuous process. Gandhiji thus does not favour an alternative model; it is neither practicable nor desirable. To quote Gopinath Dhawan, "The ideal non-violent society of Gandhiji, unattainable due to human imperfection, indicates the direction rather than, the destination, the process rather than the consummation". The Gandhian alternative is thus no rigid model, but it is a process.

The closeness between religion and politics did not mean that there was a subordination of the State to any church. In fact, Indian political thought was not affected by anything like the church-State struggle in the West. It was Asoka who brought in the notion of a non-sectarian, secular State in which all religions were respected and all men fused their religious and political concerns through the idea of *dharma*. Gandhiji was in accord with Indian tradition in rejecting the modern dichotomy between religion and politics. He rejected the possibility of any conflict, in the ultimate analysis, between political expediency and moral principles derived from religious conviction.

6

SATYAGRAHA IN SOUTH AFRICA

The *Satyagraha* struggle of the Indians in South Africa lasted for eight years. It is very remarkable that Gandhiji was a creative leader and made a synthesis of the diverse and different stands of thought in some fields and in some others, he broke new ground. Future generations will particularly remember Gandhiji for his original contribution i.e., use of non-violent methods and rejection of violence for the resolution of social and political conflicts. He will also be remembered for combining theory with practice, individual religious outlook with life-affirmation, morality with public activity, advocating non-cooperation with evil along with adherence to non-violence without malice towards the opponents.

The first and foremost challenging situations in South Africa developed in 1893, when Gandhiji travelled in a train in the first class compartment, since he had paid the amount for and had a first class ticket. When the train recahed Maritzburg, the capital of Natal at 9 p.m., one European passenger, who entered the train objected to the so-called Coolie Gandhiji, an Indian, travelling in the same compartment with him. On his complaint, a railway official asked Gandhiji to go to the van compartment. But Gandhiji refused to do so on the ground that he had a first class ticket. Then a police constable was brought who pushed out Gandhiji from the first class compartment. So, Gandhiji was constrained to spend the whole right on the platform in the shivering cold, since his overcoat was in the luggage which was with the railway official. It is significant that this was the first civil resistance that he performed and it was only the beginning of the historic and epic struggles that Gandhiji launched in South Africa.

Gandhiji visited South Africa in 1893 as a barrister to appear before the court on behalf of his client, Mr. Abdullah, who was of Indian origin. His plan was to return to India, after completing his work connected with the civil suit. However, on the eve of his return to India, he came across a news item in the *Natal Mercury* giving details of a Bill which was aimed at disenfranchising the Indians. Gandhiji was greatly agitated and he started thinking seriously about the plight of his countrymen in South Africa. He postponed his return to India at first for one month. Later on, he decided to stay for a longer period and led a campaign against the Bill. In the middle of 1896, he came to India to take his family to South Africa and he made use of his presence in India to give wide publicity to the cause of Indians in South Africa. On his return to South Africa in 1897, a Eruopean crowd at Durban attempted to lynch him.

It is interesting to note that two classes of Indians settled in Natal i.e., free traders and their free servants and secondly indentured labourers. The first batch of indentured labourers from India reached Natal on 16 November, 1860—truly a fateful day in the history of South Africa. Had it not been for this event, there would have been no Indians and therefore no *Satyagraha* in South Africa. Indeed, the steamer which carried those labourers to Natal carried with them the seed of the great *Satyagraha* movement. No adequate provisions are made as to how these illiterate and helpess labourers, who went to a distant land, were to seek redress, if they had legitimate and just grievances. The labourers went to Natal under indenture for a period of five years. After the expiry of that period, they were entitled to work as free labourers or trade in Natal and settle there if they wished. But they were not admitted to have all the rights and they were required to obtain a pass if they wanted to go from one place to another; and if their marriages were to be recognised, they were required to register with an official known as protector of Indian immigrants. An annual Poll Tax of twenty-five pounds or 375 rupees was imposed on every Indian who was freed from indenture. After great and powerful agitations, the tax was reduced to 3 pounds.

In 1894, a Bill based on the principle of excluding Indians from the franchise, the first piece of legislation based on racial distinction, was introduced in the Legislative Assembly of Natal. A memorial with ten thousand signatures was submitted to Lord Ripon, who was then Secretary of State for the colonies, and peaceful agitation was carried on against the Natal Government. Lord Ripon disallowed the bill and declared that the British Empire could not agree to the establishment of colour bar in legislation. This was indeed a great victory for the Indians. Later on, by two other laws passed by the Natal legislation, inspite of great resistance offered by Indians severe restrictions were imposed on Indian traders and no one could trade without a licence; another law was the Indian Immigration Act which closed the doors of Natal against crores of Indians, except those who were able to pass the education test in a European language. In the same manner, in other countries like the Transvaal and Cape colony, drastic laws were passed on racial discrimination. In 1885, as per the terms of Law 3, every Indian settling in the Transvaal for the purpose of carrying on the trade was required to be registered at a cost of 25 pounds otherwise subject to heavy penalties, and no Indians could hold an inch of land or enjoy the rights of citizenship. When there was great opposition the Law was amended in 1886 and the registration fees was reduced to 3 pounds and Indians could own property in such locations, wards, and streets as were specially set apart for their residence, by the Transvaal Government.

All his personal experiences in South Africa, particularly at Maritzburg, Pardeburg, Pretoria, Johannesburg and Durban prepared Gandhiji slowly and steadily along the lines of *Satyagraha* and fitted him to lead the mass movement in South Africa. The important incident that happened at Pardeburg in 1893 is worth studying, since it contained all the seeds and elements of his future *Satyagraha* movements. On one occasion, he had to travel in a coach and he purchased a first class ticket and yet he had to sit outside by the side of the coachman. He had not only a right to sit where he was sitting, but he had a right even to sit inside the coach. So, truth and justice and fair play were the factors in his favour. But, the coach-guard asked him to get down and sit at his feet. Gandhiji refused and so the guard began to belabour him. In such circumstances he could have struck a blow or two. But he did not since his method of resistance was different. He did not even abuse him, nor did he wish him ill. Upto the end, he stuck on to his seat and suffered at the hands of an erring brother, without retaliation or ill-will. Then the passengers intervened and the beatings stopped. Gandhiji acted like a true *Satyagrahi*. He once remarked that it was in the family life that he practised lessons of *Satyagraha*. He said, I learnt the lesson of non-violence of *Satyagraha* from my wife. I tried to bend her to my will. Her determined resistance to my will on one side and her quiet submission to the suffering from my stupidity, involved on the other side, ultimately made me ashamed of myself and cured me of my stupidity in thinking that I was born to rule over her and in the end she became my teacher in non-violence. And what I did in South Africa was but an extension of *Satyagraha* she unwittingly practised in her own prison".

The decision to start *Satyagraha* in South Africa came to Gandhiji suddenly. He said, "As though unknown to me, the vow of *brahmacharya* has been preparing me for *Satyagraha*. It was not a pre-conceived plan and it came on spontaneously without my having willed it'. He took the vow of *brahmacharya* in Phoenix. To a question, as to how Gandhiji began his *Satyagraha* movement, asked by the Doke, Gandhiji gave the following answer. "Some years ago when I began to take an active part in the public life of Natal, the adoption of this method occurred to me, as the best course, should petitions fail. . . . In Johannesburg when the Asiatic Registration Act was introduced the Indian community was so deeply stirred and so knit together in a common determination to resist it that moment seemed opportune . . . their action should not take a riotous form, but that of passive resistance. They had no vote in Parliament, no hope of obtaining redress, no one would listen to their complaints. The Christian churches were also indifferent. So, I proposed this pathway of suffering and after much discussion, it was adopted. This vivid and clear description of the origin of the South Africa *Satyagraha* is very important historically and as an epoch making event, since it is the oldest and also the most authentic and it is recorded by the author of the movement, soon after it started".

On 11 September, 1906, a big meeting was held and it was attended by delegates from various places in the Transvaal. Abdul Ghani, Chairman of the Transvaal British Indian Association presided over the famous fourth resolution by which the Indians solemnly determined not to submit to the ordinance; when it became the obnoxious law inspite of their great opposition, it was also decided that they must all suffer all the penalties attached to such non-submission. He fully explained the above resolution and Sheth Haji Habib declared in the name of God that he would never submit to that law and advised all present to do likewise. The workers did not let the grass grow under their feet. After the great meeting, many further meetings were held in important places and pledges of resistance were taken in every place and main topic of discussion in Indian Opinion was the Black Ordinance. A deputation waited on Mr. Duncan, the Colonial Secretary and Sheth Haji Habib, one of the members of the deputation declared, "I will not at all restrain myself, if any officer comes and proceeds to take my wife's finger prints, I will kill him there and then die myself".

When the Asiatic Department was in an irksome and awkward position, since the department could not get more than five hundred Indians willing to register, the officials decided to arrest some Indians and the first *Satyagrahi* prisoner was Rama Sundaram; Anxious Indian spectators filled the court room and Rama Sundaram was sentenced to one month's simple imprisonment and was kept in a separate cell in the European ward in Johannesburg jail. The government failed to reap any advantage form Rama Sundaram's arrest, since there were no voluntary registrations and the spirit and tempo of resistance from the Indian community rose rapidly. The Black Act applied to the Chinese as well as to the Indians. So, the Chinese joined in large numbers in the *Satyagraha* struggle and they worked through their own independent organisation. On 10th January, 1908, the last date for registration or to leave the Transvaal, Gandhiji and others were asked to attend the court. He requested the Magistrate to impose the heaviest penalty on him. The Magistrate, however, did not accede to his request and sentenced him to two month's imprisonment; this was the first imprisonment suffered by Gandhiji in the movement started by him. Gradually the number of *Satyagrahi* prisoners rose to over one hundred and fifty. After two or three days Mr. Cartwright came to see Gandhiji in the jail and brought with him the terms of settlement drafted and approved by General Smuts. On 30th January, 1908, Vernon, the Superintendent of Police in Johannesburg took Gandhiji to Pretoria to meet General Smuts. According to the terms of the first settlement, the Government agreed to repeal the Black Act, if the Indians agreed to voluntary registration. Gandhiji consulted his fellow prisoners, and Thambi Naidoo and Lening Quinn, including Gandhiji signed the draft. After the historic meeting with General Smuts, Gandhiji asked the General, "Where am I to go? And what about the other prisoners?" General Smuts laughed and said, "You are free this very moment. I am phoning to the prison officials to release the other prisoners tomorrow morning'".

Instead of repealing the Black Act, General Smuts took a fresh step forward and maintained the Black Act on the statute book and also introduced into the Legislature a measure validating the voluntary registrations. In this way, there came into force two concurrent pieces of legislation with one and the same object. Thus, as Gandhiji expressed, there was clearly breach of faith on the part of General Smuts, and Gandhiji was simply astounded, when he read the bill and did not know how he could face the Indian community. A strongly worded ultimatum was sent to the

Government and it stated clearly, "It is well known that the Indians have registered voluntarily, to the satisfaction of the government and therefore the Asiatic Act must be repealed. The community has sent many communications to General Smuts and taken all possible legal steps to obtain redress but thus far to no purpose. At a time when the bill is passing through the legislative, it is upto the leader to appraise the government of the discontent and strong feelings prevalent in the community. We regret to state that if the Asiatic Act is not repealed in terms of the settlement and if the government's decision to the effect is not communicated to the Indians before a specific date, the certificates collected by the Indians would be burnt and they would humbly but firmly take the consequences".

Since there was no reply from the government, on 16 August 1908, exactly at four O'clock, on the grounds of the Hamidia Mosque in Johannesburg, every inch of space available was taken up by Indians of all classes. The committee already received more than 2000 certificates to be burnt. It is interesting to note that Mir Alam too was present at the meeting. Mir Alam was an old client of Gandhiji. He did not like Gandhiji's decision to voluntarily register under the Asiatic Registration Act as agreed upon with General Smuts. Mir Alam severely beat Gandhiji but Gandhiji put up with a smile on his face. Mir Alam was arrested but Gandhiji did not file a complaint against him and saw to it that he was released. He announced that he committed a great wrong by assaulting Gandhiji and to the great joy of the audience, handed over his original certificate to be burnt. Gandhiji took hold of Mir Alam's hand, pressed it with joy and assured him once more that he had never harboured in his mind any resentment against him. In so doing Gandhiji followed the noble principle, "To err is human and to forgive is Divine" and also displayed the true spirit and inherent nature of a true *Satyagraha*. All the certificates were thrown into the cauldron saturated with paraffin and set ablaze by Mr. Essop Mian. The whole asssembly rose to their feet and made the place resound with the echoes of their thundering and continuous cheers during the burning process. Some members who still withheld their certificates brought them to the platform and those certificates were also consigned to the flames to the great joy of the audience. Johannesburg correspondent of the *Daily Mail* of London sent a vivid description of the meeting and compared the act of the Indians in burning their certificates with that of the Boston Tea Party.

Any account of the *Satyagraha* movement in South Africa, would be incomplete and to that extent imperfect if the great sacrifices made by the following personalities were not detailed in these pages. It is very remarkable that in the movement, Hindus, Muslims, Parsis and Christians worked harmoniously and came together as members of a well-knit family, and traders, educated men and others performed excellently the duties assigned to them. Sorabji, as the name itself suggest was a Parsi gentleman and there were more than one hundred Parsis in South Africa. Sorabji was a barrister and after being called to the bar in England, returned to Johannesburg to practice law and also to serve the Indian community. When Sorabji entered the Transvaal, the magistrate ordered him to leave the Transvaal within seven days, and on his refusal to do so, he was brought to the court on 20 July, 1908 and sentenced to one month's imprisonment with hard labour. Sheth Daud Mahomed was the President of the Natal Indian Congress and was also one of the oldest Indian traders in South Africa. When Sheth Daud arrived on the frontiers of the Transvaal with his *Satyagraha* army, they were all arrested and on 18 August 1908, they were all brought before the magistrate who ordered them to leave the Transvaal within seven days. They disobeyed the order and were rearrested at Pretoria and deported without trial. They re-entered the Transvaal on 31 August, 1908, and so they were sentenced to a fine of 50 pounds or 3 month's imprisonment with hard labour. They refused to pay the fines and cheerfully entered into the jails. Joseph Royappan, another barrister of Cambridge University was born in Natal of parents who were indentured labourers. He left his law books and took up a basket of vegetables and was arrested as an unlicensed hawker and suffered imprisonment.

It is very remarkable that many lads—sixteen years old went to jail and one lad by name Mohanlal Mauji Ghelani was only fourteen years old and thus proved that in the movement, youngsters also took an active part, courted arrest and went to jail cheerfully. The jail authorities left no stone unturned to harass the Indian prisoners; they were given scavenger's work and they did it with a smile on their faces. When they were asked to break stones, they broke stones with the name of Allah or Rama on their lips and willingly underwent all sorts of sufferings without any ill-will or malice towards the authorities, as true *Satyagrahis*. In short, the obnoxious legislation provided for three kinds of punishment i.e., fine, imprisonment and deportation. The courts were empowered simultaneously to award all the punishments and all magistrates were given jurisdiction to impose the maximum penalties.

There were special prisons where dangerous prisoners or prisoners whom the government wanted to bend, were kept and one such prison was Diepklo of convict prison. There was a harsh jailer in charge of this prison house and the labour extracted from prisoners was also very hard. The prisoners were prepared to work hard. but they would not put up with the insults hurled at them by the jailer and so they went on hunger strike for the first time in the history of Transvaal jails. They refused to take food, until the jailer was removed or they themselves were transferred to another prison. After a seven days fast, they succeeded in getting themselves transferred to another prison. As hunger strikes were very rare in those days, these *Satyagrahis* deserved special praise and entitled to special credit as pioneers in the hunger-struggle. Gandhiji was also arrested again and imprisoned in Volkrust jail. There were nearly seventy five Indian prisoners in that jail. They cooked their own food and Gandhiji became the chief cook, as he alone could adjudicate on the conflicting claims to the rations supplied. After some days the government thought that if they separated Gandhiji from other prisoners, it might perhaps chasten or reform Gandhiji as well as others, so Gandhiji was taken to Pretoria jail and was confined in a solitary cell reserved for dangerous prisoners.

The caravan of pilgrims consisted of 2037 men, 127 women and 57 children and at the appointed stroke of the hour i.e., at 6.30 a.m. on 6 November 1913 the members offered prayers and commenced their historic march in the name of God. A small patrol of mounted policemen was on duty at the border gate. Gandhiji went up to them, leaving instructions with the members to cross over when he signalled to them. While he was still talking to the police, the pilgrims made a sudden rush and crossed the border. The police surrounded them, but had no intention of arresting them. Gandhiji pacified the pilgrims and got them to arrange themselves in regular rows. Everything was in order in a few minutes and the march into the Transvaal began. One European challenged Mr. Kallenbach to a duel who replied in the following immortal words in the meeting of the Europeans. "The Indians are not out to challenge your position as ruler. They do not wish to fight with you or to fill the country. They only seek justice, pure and simple. They propose to enter the Transvaal not with a view to settle there, but only as an effective demonstration against the unjust tax which is levied upon them. They are brave men. They will not injure you in person or in property. They will not fight with you, but enter the Transvaal they will, even in the face of your gunfire. They are not the men to beat a retreat from the fear of bullets or your spears. They propose to melt, and I know they will melt, your hearts by false suffering". The audience was rather abashed and the gentleman who invited Mr. Kallenbach to single combat became his friend.

On the first day, they stopped for the night at Palmford about eight miles from the Transvaal. Late in the night. Gandhiji was arrested and was taken to the nearest railway station. Before accompanying the police officer, Gandhiji informed P.K. Naidoo about his arrest and told him that at day-break, the pilgrims must regularly resume their march. Gandhiji was produced before a Magistrate in Volkrust and the case was postponed; on Gandhiji's request the Magistrate released him on bail of 50 pounds. So Gandhiji joined the caravan of pilgrims in their march. Gandhiji was re-arrested at Standerton and by the time he reached the court-room, he found that five of his co-workers, including P.K. Naidoo were arrested and remained in jail. Gandhiji was again released on bail of 50 pounds. When the pilgrims reached Teakworth, the principal immigration officer of the Transvaal and a police officer arrested Gandhiji, and thus he was arrested thrice in four days; he was taken to Heidelberg and from there to Dundee where he was tried and sentenced to nine months imprisonment with hard labour. The pilgrims with Polak as their leader resumed their march and halted for the night at Creylingstad. When all the pilgrims reached Balfour on the tenth at about 9 O'Clock, the special trains were drawn up at the station to take them and depart them to Natal. Later on, Gandhiji was separated from his friends in jail and was lodged in a solitary cell in Bleomfontin jail; Kellenbach was taken to Pretoria jail and Polak to Germiston jail.

In December 1913, Lord Hardinge, the Viceroy of India made his famous speech in Madras which created a great stir and commotion in South Africa as well as in England. Lord Hardinge not only passed the criticism on the Union Government, but he also whole-heartedly defended the action of the *Satyagrahis* and supported their civil disobedience of unjust amd invidious legislation. Like New Castle in the mine area, Phoenix too became the centre of the strikers on the north coast. As soon as the arrest of Mr. West was cabled to Gokhale, he initiated the policy of sending able men from India and so Andrews and Pearson left India for South Africa by the first available steamer. The Union Government had not the power to keep thousands of innocent men in jail for ever. The wrong perpetrated was well known to all and everyone realised that it must be redressed. At last, it dawned on the philosopher-statesman, General Smuts, that there had been injustice which called for remedy. As usual, a commission was appointed to submit a detailed report to the Union Government.

On the recommendation of the commission, Kallenbach, Polak and Gandhiji were released unconditionally and simultaneously on 18th December 1913, after an imprisonment of hardly six weeks Mr. West was also released from jail, as the Government had no case against him. All these events took place before the arrival of Andrews and Pearson whom Gandhiji was able to welcome as they landed at Durban. Later on, Gandhiji went to Pretoria with Andrews and just at that time, there was a great strike of the European employees of the Union Railways which made the position of the Government extremely delicate. Supporters of Gandhiji suggested that the new struggle or the Indian march should be commenced at such a fortunate juncture. But, on moral grounds Gandhiji declined to do so. General Smuts said, "I do not like your people and do not care to assist them at all. But, what am I to do? You help us in our days of need. How can we lay hands upon you? I often wish you took to violence like the English strikes and then, we would know at once how to dispose of you. But you will not injure even the enemy. You desire victory by self-suffering alone and never transgress your self-imposed limits of courtesy and chivalry and that is what reduces to us to sheer helplessness".

Andrews and Gandhiji had frequent interviews with General Smuts before letters were exchanged and at last a provisional agreement was reached and the *Satyagraha* movement was suspended and the agreement was endorsed by the Indians. The boycott of the commission by the *Satyagraha* volunteers did not produce any bad effect. On the other hand, its work was shortened and its report was published soon and the report of the commission was favourable to the Indians, as predicted by General Smuts. Within a short time of the issue of the report, the Government published in the official Gazette of the Union the Indian Relief Bill which contained nine sections. One part of it dealt with the question of Indian Marriages and validated in South Africa the marriages which were held legal in India, except that if a man had more wives than one, only one of them would at any time be recognised as his legal wife in South Afirica. The second part abolished the annual licence of three pounds, while the third part dealt with the domicile certificates issued by the Government to Indians in Natal. In short, with the passing of the Indian Relief Bill and the correspondence between Gandhiji and General Smuts finally ended the *satyagraha* struggle which commenced in September 1906 and lasted for eight long years and the Indians in South Africa could live in peace and tranquillity. On 18 July 1914, Gandhiji sailed for England, on his way back to India, with mixed feelings of pleasure and regret—pleasure because he was returning home after many years and anxiously looked forward to serve his motherland under Gopalakrishna Gokhale's guidance, and with regret because it was a sad moment to leave South Africa, after staying for twenty one years of his life and after having shared the joys and sorrows of his countrymen there.

Gandhiji demonstrated with success, by his historic and epoch-making non-violent movement in South Africa, that *Satyagraha* is a priceless and matchless weapon and those who wield it are strangers to defeat or disappointment. The *Satyagraha* movement in South Africa, the first mass *Satyagraha* and most important in historical perspective was launched by Gandhiji to fight against racial discrimination as well as the unjust laws of the government. The movement attracted world-wide publicity and attention. Since it was initiated and led throughout by Gandhiji, and since he practically evolved his unique and dynamic methods during his campaigns in South Africa he thus made or created new history by revolutionising the methods of fighting for social justice and equity. The *Satyagraha* movement in South Africa proved beyond doubt that the opponent's difficulty is never the Satyagrahi's opportunity and a true *Satyagrahi* would go out of his way to help the opponent in his difficulties. When the Indian employees of Durban Municipality struck work, all those who were engaged in sanitary services of the Borough and attendants on the patients in the hospitals were sent back to their duties, so that there might be no outbreak of any epidemic in the city and the sick and the wounded in the hospitals might not suffer for want of proper and timely help and services.

In short, the seeds of *Satyagraha* sown in South Africa germinated so well and blossomed forth so beautifully and victoriously and spread their sweet fragrance in India and finally crossed the Indian frontiers and spread the eternal messages of truth and non-violence, compassion and universal brotherhood that have engulfed the corridors of the world. Typically and appropriately General Smuts commented, "The saint has departed from our shores. I trust he will never return". After the *Satyagraha* movement in South Africa, all the Indians had realised their full potential. While in prison, Gandhiji made a pair of sandals and presented them to

General Smuts and he wore them for the rest of his life, since Gandhiji had made them well. Though their political relationship was strained many times, General Smuts always felt compelled to respond to any call from Gandhiji.

BIBLIOGRAPHY

Arunachalam, K., *Khadi Economics—A Few Aspects*, Koodal Publishers, Madurai, 1974.

Bharathi, K.S., *Socio-Religious Thoughts of Mahatma Gandhi*, Dattsons Publishers, Nagpur, 1989.

Bharathi, K.S., *Gandhiji and Nehru,* Indus Publishing Co., New Delhi, 1990.

Bharathi, K.S., *The Satyagraha of Mahatma Gandhi,* Indus Publishing Co., New Delhi, 1990.

Bharathi, K.S., *The Political Thought of Gandhi,* Dattsons Publishers, Nagpur, 1995.

Bondurant, J.V., *Conquest of Violence,* Oxford University Press, Bombay, 1959.

Bose, N.K., *Studies in Gandhism,* Navajeevan Publishing House, Ahmedabad, 1972.

Datta, D.M., *The Philosophy of Mahatma Gandhi*, University of Wisconsin Press, Madison, 1953.

Dhawan, G., *The Political Philosophy of Mahatma Gandhi,* Navajeevan Publishing House, Ahmedabad, 1962.

Diwakar, R.R., *Satyagraha in Action, World Pacifist Meeting*, Signet Press, Calcutta.

Dutta, D.K., *Social, Moral and Religious Philosophy of Mahatma Gandhi,* Intellectual Book Corner, New Delhi, 1980.

Fischer, L., *The Life of Mahatma Gandhi,* Harper and Brothers, New York, 1950.

Gandhi, M.K., *Hind Swaraj,* Navajeevan Publishing House, Ahmedabad, 1946.

Gandhi, M.K., *Communal Unity,* Navajeevan Publishing House, Ahmedabad, 1951.

Holmes, W.H.G., *The Twofold Gandhiji,* Mowbray and Co., London, 1952.

Iyengar, A.S., *All Through the Gandhian Era,* Hind Kitab Ltd., Bombay, 1950.

Iyer, R.N., *The Moral and Political Thought of Mahatma Gandhi*, Oxford University Press, Oxford, 1978.

Keer, D., *Gandhi: Political Saint and Unarmed Prophet*, Bombay, 1943.

Keer, D., *Mahatma Gandhi*, Popular Prakashan, Bombay, 1973.

Kumarappa, J.C., *Gandhian Thought*, Vora and Co., Bombay, 1951.

Lalkhanna, K.K., *Mahatma Gandhi Contribution to Hinduism*, Classical Publishing Company, New Delhi, 1981.

Laski, H.J., *A Grammar of Politics*, George Allen and Unwin Ltd., London, 1948.

Migabraim, U.S., *Message of Mahatma Gandhi*, Publication Division, Delhi, 1969.

Muzumdar, H.T., *Mahatma Gandhi : A Prophetic Voice*, Navajeevan Publishing House, Ahmedabad, 1963.

Nanda, B.R., *Mahatma Gandhi*, Allen and Unwin, London, 1958.

Narayan, R.S., *Gandhi's Contribution to Political Thought*, Prasaranga, University of Mysore, 1982.

Ostergaard, G., *Non-violent Revolution in India*, Gandhi Peace Foundation, New Delhi, 1985.

Patil, V.T., *Studies on Gandhi*, Sterling Publishers, New Delhi, 1983.

Power, P.F., *Gandhi on World Affairs*, George Allen and Unwin Ltd., London, 1961.

Prabhu, R.K., and U.R. Rao, *The Mind of Mahatma Gandhi*, Navajeevan Publishing House, Ahmedabad, 1967.

Prasad, R., *At the Feet of Mahatma Gandhi*, Hind Kitabs, Bombay, 1955.

Pyarelal, *Mahatma Gandhi, The Last Phase*. 2 vols., Navajeevan Publishing House, Ahmedabad, 1958.

Radhakrishnan, S., *Mahatma Gandhi : Essays and Reflections on His Life and Works*, Allen and Unwin, London, 1939.

Radhakrishnan, S., *Mahatma Gandhi : 100 Years*, Orient Longmans, Delhi, 1968.

Ramsahray, R., *Gandhi: Soundings in Political Philosophy*, Chanakya Publication, Delhi, 1984.

Ramashray, R., *Self and Society : A Study in Gandhian Thought*, Sage Publishers, New Delhi, 1984.

Rolland, R., *Mahatma Gandhi*, Allen and Unwin, London, 1924.

Rothermund, I., *The Philosophy of Restraint*, Popular Prakashan, Bombay, 1963.

Sethi, J.D., *Gandhi Today*, Vikas Publishing House, Delhi, 1978.

Sharma, B.S., *Gandhi as a Political Thinker*, Indian Press Publications Pvt. Ltd., Allahabad, 1956.

Spratt, P., *Gandhism: An Analysis*, Huxley Press, Madras, 1939.

Tandon, V., *The Social and Political Philosophy of Sarvodaya After Gandhi,* Sarva Seva Sangh Prakashan, Varanasi, 1965.

Tendulkar, D.G., *Mahatma : Life of Mohandas Karamchand Gandhi,* 8 vols., V. K. Jhaveri, Bombay, 1951-54.

Unnithan, T.K.N., *Gandhi and Social Change,* Rawat Publications, Jaipur, 1979.

Varma, V.P., *The Political Philosophy of Mahatma Gandhi and Sarvodaya,* Lakshmi Narayan Agarwal Publishers, Agra, 1972.

Watson, F., *Talking of Gandhiji,* Orient Longmans, Calcutta, 1957.

INDEX